Things I Wish I Had Taught My Son... And Still Can

JESÚS RAMÍREZ

Outskirts Press Inc. • **Denver, Colorado**

Outskirts Press, Inc.
http://www.outskirtspress.com

ISBN: 978-1-4327-5420-4

Library of Congress Control Number: 2010927448

Outskirts Press and the "OP" logo are trademarks belonging to Outskirts Press, Inc.

PRINTED IN THE UNITED STATES OF AMERICA

Things I Wish I Had Taught My Son... And Still Can is a daily email that I started sending my son when he left for college. I felt that there was so much left to pass on. I thought the medium of email would be the best way to reach him. These emails (now in book) form include life lessons, business lessons, how-to's, found wisdom, and words of encouragement for the interesting life ahead.

I am the father of eight children with a beautiful challenge at juggling life, health, family, career, entrepreneurship, etc. I believe in learning by teaching. Therefore, I invested quality time everyday writing these emails so that they could serve my oldest son, and so that they can also serve all my other children. All but the youngest three are reading along. At the prompting of some friends, I made these emails public. I got permission from my son. Now I have compiled the first 120 lessons into a book.

And the journey begins.

Table of Content

#1 THINGS I WISH I HAD TAUGHT MY SON… AND STILL CAN
The balancing act.

For 20 years I have heard of a concept which at first I didn't get. I thought it was a nice to have, not a gotta have. Reflecting back I think my unconscious did pay attention to that valuable lesson. Reflecting back, I think it is what drives me now, keeps me in check. What is that lesson that I have been learning for the better part of my adult life?

Balance.

I have suffered when I have gone to extremes in anything. Work, play, study, anything. I have been saved by my will to maintain a balance between family and work, God and science, intellect and intuition, listening and speaking, tradition and change, music and silence, light and darkness, relaxation and determination, health and leisure, etc…

Balance.

It's not a concept anymore for me. It is my context. It is the invisible framework that guides me through my day, through my life.

I had a different plan in mind on how I would impart some of my acquired wisdom. I didn't think you were interested in your high school years. Now that you are away and in a semi contemplative place where you look to define your life, I will periodically send some "things" that you can accept or reject. But at least I will have passed on something more valuable than money or material possessions.

> *Life is a classroom,*
> *Your papi*

#2 THINGS I WISH I HAD TAUGHT MY SON… AND STILL CAN
If you're not going to say something spirit building…

Don Miguel Ruiz the famous author of *The Four Agreements* calls it… "Be Impeccable with your words."

What he means is never inflict pain on anyone with your words. That's because whether positive or negative, words are powerful.

Words make or break a young child's spirit. Words break hearts. Words leave scars that hurt a lifetime.

But it seems, because people insult one another so often, we are impermeable to "put downs". Not true. The child inside of us still gets damaged when somebody cuts us down. Some people will carry the baggage of insults with them to their grave. Families have been destroyed by what seemed like a little joke.

There is a cliché that older people use. They use it because it is wisdom. They say… "If you're not going to say something good about someone, then don't say anything at all." It's not cool to insult. It's sort of like an "in" thing. But insulting is like stealing life from somebody.

Take Don Miguel Ruiz's shamanic advice and build people's spirit with your words. If a put down session is already taking place and somebody you know is the one who is being ground down to mince meat, don't participate. Don't add your two cents worth of insults. If you do participate, your "so-called" friends will expect you to be mean-spirited and they will eventually fear that mean spirit that lives and grows within you.

Word,
Your papi

 #3 THINGS I WISH I HAD TAUGHT MY SON… AND STILL CAN
When the bank is the predator…

Today I found out that your checking account is overdrawn. Remember my lesson on balance just two days ago? It applies to your checkbook too — your online account, whatever they call it these days.

Over the course of your life you will lose tens of thousands of dollars to carelessness mismanaged plans, and downright robbery from banks (Who would have thought that banks would be robbing us?). Some of your losses will be valuable learning like today. Most of it will be just waste. I'm sort of glad that you had this overdrawn lesson on the first day of college. So here goes the lesson that accompanies "balance."

We live in an information universe where you can receive your daily balance on your phone every single day of the year. I do. And you should set that up right away. You should also select all the other tools like "low balance", deductions over $$, etc. This wasn't available when I was in college, but banks weren't so predatory either. Nowadays banks want to steal your money even though they're supposed to be safekeeping it. They are not your friends. Use them and take advantage of their organizational products but never turn your back on them. They love overdrafters and disorganized customers. Fraud is now something to worry about. Pay attention to the activity on your account and help the police catch the criminals.

Unless you are diligent with your finances, you won't know, and they'll get away with your money. And as Santa, your little baby sister would say, "That's not nice!"

Checking out,
Your papi

 #4 THINGS I WISH I HAD TAUGHT MY SON... AND STILL CAN
Write... And write... And write... Until it feels right.

I've written award-winning ads and commercials. I've written songs for commercials. They used to call them jingles (a term I hated). I've written many songs for my wife, your mom. I've written a few songs for you along with your brothers and sisters to sing on Mother's Day. 12 Christian songs... Even one with you. I've written poems, which I have never shared with you. And perhaps I never will.

From 1998 to 2000, if memory serves me right, I wrote a daily email diary that I shared with my brothers, sisters and parents. I have those on some obscure backup drive stashed away.

I've written a book... A book that nobody read. Not even my wife or any of my children. When we were courting, I wrote a daily letter to my girlfriend, your mom, when I was in Austin, Texas, and she was in Laredo, Texas, and later San Antonio. She also wrote back to me every day.

And now I'm writing my *"I wish I had taught my son"* emails to you.

What you may not know is that when I was your age, I despised writing. My first three essay grades in English totaled 75 – 25 each. I thought I would be thrown out of college because I couldn't write. I had no clue about grammar. My vocabulary was pitiful. And all those ideas I had... They were trapped in my head with no possible way of jumping out to a page or a screen.

I struggled through college even though I had great grades. And I just wanted to get all my writing over with. Or so I thought.

Becoming a writer of stuff was not in my plans, but I now thank God every day that he blessed me with the ability to finally understand how to organize my thoughts into something readable.

The lesson today is that you make writing a priority. It is a time machine. A portal. A journey. A friend.

Write on!
Your papi

 #5 THINGS I WISH I HAD TAUGHT MY SON... AND STILL CAN
Make a note of this... And test yourself.

In the next few days you will be given multiple reading assignments at college. Teachers will give you a syllabus. On that syllabus will be specifics about what chapters from those books you just bought (which totaled more than $500... Ouch!), you need to read and by when you need to read them. Don't take those assignments lightly. Very soon you will find yourself taking a test where most of the subject matter came totally from those expensive books and for which none of the subject matter was ever discussed in class.

FORGET THE HIGHLIGHTER. Besides ruining your books, highlighters, the college kid's favorite "pretend you are studious" activity is completely useless. I will highlight this and underline it to make my point. Highlighters are completely useless. Instead, I suggest a different behavior. It requires more commitment but virtually guarantees your success. I learned it from your mom, and she learned it from a videotape back in the day that propelled her from a borderline C and D student to an A student.

What was the behavior? She did two things. First of all, when reading her textbooks she forced herself to make her own tests. She put her reading material into question form, literally. She pretended to be the teacher and looked for possible questions hidden in the readings (about two questions per paragraph) and then used those questions to study from before the test day. She also did something else to succeed.

TAKE NOTE... While in class she took good notes. That's a no-brainer. You have to do that. But what she did with those notes is the insight I want to pass on to you. After class, first chance she got, mom would find a quiet spot and play back in her mind what all the notes meant. She cemented her knowledge when she did this. She made it stick like Velcro. Trying to remember what you wrote down two weeks prior only puts you in a position to remember less than half of what you wrote and the context in which it was presented. So when you get out of class, find a tree to sit under or a distraction-proof seat somewhere and take a deep dive into your notes and upload them to the RAM of your mind. Then, when the time comes to review your notes and review the potential test questions from your textbooks, you won't need to cram, you'll walk in confidently and you'll kick some comosellama.

Mark my words: it'll work. Better yet, don't mark my words. Just take the advice.

Any questions?
Your papi

 #6 THINGS I WISH I HAD TAUGHT MY SON... AND STILL CAN
Handle this advice with care... Because it's hot!

Some people learn this lesson the hard way, the excruciatingly painful way, and some of the damage it causes is irreparable. Sooner then later, you and/or one of your friends will be driving down the highway, and the car will heat up. This (in case you didn't know) will destroy the vehicle if you continue to drive this way for an extended time, melting all the moldable parts that lie deep inside the engine. So lets's say you decide to pull over at a gas station and drop in the obligatory quarter or 50¢ for water into the Air/Water machine. You and your friend pop the hood of the car (once you finally find out how to do that). And both of you debate on what needs to be done.

Meanwhile the car is making strange noises. It's angry. And the pressure is building under the radiator cap. What do you do?

First of all, don't try to unscrew the radiator cap. If you do, all the pent up highly pressurized steaming and scalding water mixed with anti-freeze will shoot out at you and burn your skin. I know several people today who still carry scars from a similar incident. Most of the time, if you shut off the car, the pressure will continue to build for a while. So don't trust it then either. Opening the cap then will also end up in disaster. Only time will cool the car down.

So what do you do?

You pour the water over the outside of the radiator, in the front of the radiator, on the top and sides. Do this liberally and don't rush it. What this will do is regulate the temperature and allow all the hot water to cool down a bit. Either way, it would be wise to turn the car off and let it cool down for several hours if that is an option.

Most, if not all cars, have a reserve bin where water is stored. You should check that bin to make sure it reads "full". It has a suggested level for when the car is cold and for when it is hot. This water leaves the reserve bin (is siphoned out) during the course of the vehicle's operation. The water's role is to cool the engine, return to the radiator to be cooled by the air generated from the velocity of the vehicle and by the fan. It then cycles back to the engine. Overheating happens when this cycle is interrupted either by a lack of water or because a little regulator called the thermostat is no longer working properly.

Ouch,
Your papi

PS: Are you writing questions down while reading your assignments? Don't blow this advice off. It'll make a difference.

✉ **#7 THINGS I WISH I HAD TAUGHT MY SON… AND STILL CAN**
Your life's soundtrek…

So you're walking through campus, and you meet a girl… What's the song playing in the background?

I've always felt like I was in a movie. Even before Walkman's (do you know what those are?) and iPods, I carried music in my head that I felt fit the circumstances. Sometimes I hummed under my breath as I strutted. When I graduated from college, I decided that I would always have a running soundtrack of my life. I would actually choose what songs would be on the screen during the final credits of my "life movie". I believed they served as my signature. I would consider including the instrumentals that would take me from scene to scene… And I would include songs with a message too (Later, I'll tell you about how *The Cats in the Cradle* always haunted me…).

Over the years I have gone through genres of music exploring the widest ranges of ethnic vibes, electronic experimentation and classical remixes. I have thoroughly enjoyed my exotic musical journey. I have watched, or rather listened to the musical voyage you have been on. I hope that I have rubbed off some of that curiosity and passion I share for innovative music.

I now have the rare and unique privilege of sharing a work space with a music producer, McCumba, who is making a new piece of music "from his heart" almost everyday. I hear songs being dreamt up from the germ of the idea to the finished, polished mix. Excellent stuff. One day McCumba hypnotizes me with his prolific Jazz piano ability, and the next day he sounds like Timbaland's producer. I'm witnessing how happy he is to just write one more song today.

So have you thought of your soundtrack? Is it all one genre? Is there stuff from you childhood? Does *Blue's Clues* make the cut? Has having a soundtrack ever crossed your mind? I suggest you consider your soundtrack because it will bring you much joy later.

Looking back on the albums of my life, I think my life always sounded good.

> *Sounding off,*
> *Your papi*

PS: Your mom's and my song is *Just You and I* by Eddie Rabbit. It's on our greatest hits remix.

PSS: I just recently found out that your mom never liked this song. Instead, she liked a Bryan Adams song from the '80s.

✉ #8 THINGS I WISH I HAD TAUGHT MY SON... AND STILL CAN
Finding you...

Now that you're in college, some of your professors won't only teach about what's outside you. Some will teach about and probe deeply into what's inside you, specifically inside your mind, your heart.

So who are you? Do you know? Do you have the ability to look at yourself from the outside looking in?

Finding you is a lifelong process, but it seems that college really throws you headfirst into this discovery. Finding you will require reflecting on all the choices you've made, taking inventory of all your successes and shortcomings, and considering where you came from. You'll have to consider who your mother is, who your father is. You'll have to find a piece of your puzzle in each of your grandparents. And you'll have to understand how the schools you went to have shaped you. You'll also have to weigh in on how your culture, neighborhood, part of town, socioeconomic level, social clubs, athletic teams, coaches, teachers, brothers, sisters, groups of friends, girlfriends, confidence (or lack thereof), physical development, scolding, praises, stress level and an even longer list of emotional guideposts shaped you to get a clearer picture.

Whew! So who are you?

When you find out, let me know?

When I find out who I am, I'll let you know.

> *Your papi*

#9 THINGS I WISH I HAD TAUGHT MY SON… AND STILL CAN
What will you base your relationships on?

Today is Sunday, and I'm not going to ask you if you went to church. Mom will probably nag you about it, but not I. This is the part of your life when you go to church because you want to for yourself. Although we have provided ample examples of a living church in our lives, in our family, in our friendships, still you must decide if it is for you now or maybe later.

But I will ask you this.

When you meet that special someone, on what will this relationship be based? If it is anything other than Christ, I suggest it will be temporary. If you base the relationship on "good looks" then when those "good looks" change, the relationship will wobble on shaky ground. If the relationship is based on power or money, when that runs out, the chances of collapse will also be just around the corner. If the relationship is based on good emotions, great conversation or strong physical attraction, then too a similar fate will await you.

The only lasting thing you can base your relationship on is Jesus Christ. It is like an insurance policy for that relationship. Otherwise, it'll just drift. And eventually disintegrate.

On our wedding invitation I wrote the following words: "Through Christ, we met. Through Christ we learned to love, we learned to share. Through Christ we will be united forever." I think that because of this idea, your mom and I have been able to weather storms better than others. We've had a couple of financial collapses, we've aged, and we've even had differences of opinion on many issues. But "through Christ, we will be united forever" is a very real possibility. I know I want her next to me when I am on my death bed.

And ultimately, that is the question every couple seeking to spend the rest of their lives together should answer: "Who do you want to be next to you on your death bed?"

> *I love your mami,*
> *Your papi*

 #10 THINGS I WISH I HAD TAUGHT MY SON… AND STILL CAN
It's about time…

You've probably experienced different kinds of time already. You've experienced the 0.7 seconds at the end of the game where you or one of your teammates inbounded the ball and released the shot in time for the winning shot. Or perhaps you were on the losing end of that shot. You've experienced the longest minute when your hurt and angry mom talked to you about how you disappointed her. You may have experienced time standing still during a kiss or during a near 90° roller-coaster drop.

For some people, time flies all the time. For others it crawls. For some people time is on their side. For others, time is the enemy. For the person who is terminally ill, time is precious. For the chronic drunk, time is a thief.

For me, writing to you right now… Time is a treasure that will be frozen and preserved long after I die.

Your brother Uriel just walked in and came directly towards me. I hugged him and time shifted.

The lesson today is that you should always respect time. It is fleeting but you have exactly the same amount of time as anybody else who will accomplish more than you and as those who will scratch their heads and wonder where you found the time to accomplish so much.

Just like the passages in Ecclesiastes (3:1-8), there is a time for everything, and perhaps someday you'll feel like your time has come.

Over the years, I've learned to make time. No, I don't have a time machine. I've just tried to spend my time proactively. If you ever noticed, I seldom sat in front of the TV for long periods of time. And I will add that my time has been lucid because I rarely dulled my senses with alcohol.

Since you won't be able to hold on to time, I hope that you instead make the most out of time that you can.

Now it's time to close this. And send it through time.

Your papi

 **#11 THINGS I WISH I HAD TAUGHT MY SON… AND STILL CAN
Have you Googled something lately?**

Sooner or later you're going to be making a website for yourself, for a group you're teaming up with or for a business. And even though you're looking at a science career, you'll inevitably end up needing to understand how to make money in that chosen career. Perhaps you'll be the next Jacques Yves Cousteau or the next Crocodile Hunter, and people will come to view your latest webisodes on your website. If you end up a veterinarian or a paleontologist or an expert on plankton (not the character on *Spongebob Square Pants*), you'll need to announce to the world your services, your findings, your point-of-view, the compelling "why" they should care about your work.

Therefore, I want you to know in general terms how Google works. It is by far the most powerful search engine in the world. And since you will want people to stumble onto your site someday, you'll need to know how the logical "robots" at Google think and operate.

When you type in a combination of words in a Google search and hit enter, Google runs off throughout the world (in a matter of milliseconds) and tries to satisfy your wish, attempting to retrieve for you the best Internet website that it rationalizes will satisfy your search request. And voilà… You get a list of ranked sites that seem to be quite impressive — saving you a ton of time.

There are three main categories of results that show up on a search. There are the paid Sponsored Links on top, the top ranked unpaid sites below, and the paid Google Adword ads on the right side.

First, a little about the paid sites: These are people or companies who have bought Google Adwords. They have paid to hopefully get your attention. They are on the right side of the page on the other side of a little blue line. There are also some paid or Sponsored Links on the top of the results page usually with a light coloration. These too are paid for by individuals or companies. The prices for those ads may range from a nickel per click to quite expensive depending on the demand for those words.

The remaining results are unpaid sites that have succeeded at becoming the best ranked sites on the subject you just searched. Sometimes, they're just what you were looking for; sometimes you have to have to go deep into the other pages until you find what you wanted.

Well… Google is paying attention to your behavior. If you're not picking the sites on the first page, Google is demoting the sites on the first page. If you do find what you were looking for on the first page, Google is happy. But Google makes sure that you click on several pages within the site you enter before it deems the site a success. If you find what you were looking for on the third page of the search result listings, then Google will reward the site you pick on that third page and move them up the ranks, perhaps to the first page (if others like you also find the same site relevant).

How does Google know to even display these sites in the first place? What is Google looking for? That'll be covered in tomorrow's "things".

The bottom line… If you make a site, you'll want to be on the first page of a Google search and to do that you'll need to know what word combinations people are using to find what they're looking for. I'll let you know how that works too. But later.

Now get back to studying,
Your papi

 #12 THINGS I WISH I HAD TAUGHT MY SON… AND STILL CAN
This might make your head a little Googly… (Sorry in advance)

So I gave you an overview of the search result screen on Google in the last email. But how does Google know to find those sites for you?

Something that you will learn in any field of study, interest or business is that there will always exist a specialized language for everything. Lawyers have one. Accountants have one. Religions have one. Movie makers, theirs is really complicated. Even basketball players have a lingo. Where there are small cultures of people communicating there will be an accompanying language, a code.

In the computer world, there is also a standard language that is evolving every day. Actually what I write today about Google may be obsolete in a few months because everything is in flux.

But what is the governing language that Google uses (at least for now) for search results? It is partly the language of meta and partly the language of the "content" of the site. Let me explain. To surf the Internet, you use a browser like Firefox (Safari, Explorer, Camino and I imagine soon-to-come-to-the-Apple world, the new Google Chrome). In one of the pull-down menus in any of these browsers there is a command called something like View Page Source or View Source. Here you will find what is "under the hood" of a website. In all that garble of letters you will find something called "meta name" an "=" sign and the word "keywords" in quotes. The words that follow this are the keywords that the site you are looking at is screaming out to Google so that it gets noticed — That along with the words that follow this term, "meta name = "description". Did that make any sense? To review, what I have explained so far is that Google considers the data found in the meta name "keywords" and meta name "descriptions" to rank a site.

Where you see "title" will be the actual title that shows at the very top of your browser screen. This is usually grey and right above the URL of the site blank (the place where you type www.yahoo.com or www.google.com). Google also considers what's here because this is actually the text that shows up in blue and underlined when you conduct a Google search.

The last thing I believe that Google checks for is the actual text in the body of the website page. If the "keywords" a website maker (like myself) puts in the meta tags does not have a relationship to the actual text on the page, then the Google police punishes you and pushes you to the back of the line. Google doesn't reward people who are pretending to be content providers and who are trying to manipulate the system.

So in the end... The top-ranked Google sites are not really the best sites on a subject even though we think they are. They are just the sites with the best understanding of how to manipulate the Google robots into thinking they are the best sites. There are entire companies that go around charging big bucks for this information. And many people make a grand living off this tidbit of information. I just thought I would pass it on to you.

> *Googling out,*
> *Your papi*

PS: If you put the terms "Latino marketing" in the Google search blank and hit return, my site will be the #1 unpaid site (in the world) that shows up. Check it out for yourself. I used the principles explained above to accomplish this.

 #13 THINGS I WISH I HAD TAUGHT MY SON... AND STILL CAN
Your identity crisis... And your open sesame.

Even before your first day of college, your identity and credit card info was stolen. And the person or persons who violated your world (charging up $500) sent you on a roller-coaster of overdrafting loops and a slamming into of multiple overdraft charges.

Welcome to a world of SPAM (not the college food), digital piracy, hacking, urban legend, fraudulent e-commerce websites posing as eBay.com and Facebook.com (when these posers are actually identity thieves).

And welcome to people waiting for you to walk away from your computer (to get a snack) or watching you from across the lobby (with their built-in laptop camera) as you input your student ID password at a kiosk or your ATM pin at the dispensing machine. Sorry that I'm being a little overcompensating, but I just had my computer with about five years of work and dreams (for which I had no backup) stolen from us (and it was in a ritzy part of San Antonio). So what's the lesson?

First of all, you have to come up with a robust password for your computer. A different one for you phone. A different one for your student ID password. A different on for your bank account. And just in case you didn't know, your computer has something called Lojack for Computers.

If your computer is stolen, the Lojack for Computers headquarters will try to pinpoint the IP address of where your computer is being used, alert the police, issue a warrant and have the perpetrators arrested. However, if they crack your computer password before that (because you didn't heed my warning), then they can inflict much ID Theft damage and dump the computer somewhere before the police officers arrives.

How do you make a solid password? You include several uppercase letters, several lowercase letters and at least two numbers. Preferably the uppercase and lowercase letters are not next to each other and the numbers are also separated. 2sAnmArcos3 is an example of this. (This is San Marcos with only the "A's" capitalized and nestled within Michael Jordan's number, 23) You can still remember it with a little pattern, but it's not too obvious. But please don't use the example. Come up with one of your own.

Because I set up your computer in a hurry, I didn't get to password-protect the screen. You need to go to system preferences and instruct the computer go to sleep after five minutes of inactivity. When you touch the trackpad to wake the computer, you'll need to input your unique password. A drag, yes... But it will be a blessing if it gets stolen. Don't ever give your password to anyone. I have never given you mine. If you do end up giving yours out (because it was unavoidable) change it to something else immediately.

If a website ever asks you to select an identity question, avoid subjects that are easy to find out like the name of your dog. A predator with a little bit of Facebook information can call our home portraying to be a vet hospital and ask mom what the name of our pets are and she may volunteer it. If not, one of your brother's will proudly and happily spit it out.

Finally, never think that your dorm is a safe place to keep things. During orientation, the campus police chief told us himself that anything not tied down will get stolen in the dorms. And as for your friend's cars... the chief said and I quote... "They'll break into your car around here to steal the lose change in your ashtray."

Other than that... There's nothing to worry about.

> Logging out,
> Your papi

✉ #14 THINGS I WISH I HAD TAUGHT MY SON... AND STILL CAN
The power of the presentation...

You'll be making presentations in college... And you'll be making presentations the rest of your life on all kinds of subjects.

Your best presentations will transfer confidence. Your worst presentations will remove confidence. You won't be able to transfer confidence easily if you don't have "it", feel "it".

So how can you increase "it"?

Preparedness will help make you more confident, but you'll have to know the ins and outs of the subject you are talking about. Knowing your audience will help you because you'll be able to tailor the message you are trying to get across more relevantly. As for what to wear, I won't be giving you fashion advice here... We're living in a day where the grunge-dressed kid (because he was underestimated) now blows the audience away, while the executive in the suit can gently put everybody to sleep (because he was so painfully predictable and overestimated).

Be mildly unpredictable when you present. Audiences appreciate not knowing what is next. Our human brains only pay attention to what is interesting and unpredictable. Plus, we love to be whisked to another realm (another time and place) for a few minutes. That's why we feel great after a strangely unpredictable movie and feel cheated when we could predict every scene, twist and turn of a cinematic bomb.

Some presentations are enhanced with props. I once used a lava lamp to make a point. I'm a master at using animation inside PowerPoint and Keynote applications. I've invented my own brand of "how did you do that?" presentations. And because I have shot thousands of hours of video and have learned to edit gracefully, I can transfer confidence through the use of my short movie presentations. I suspect I will reprise on this subject of "the presentation" but I'll close this one right here.

And to add a cherry on top to this email... Check out a presentation I put together of your Three-Point prowess. You look pretty confident in this presentation. Click the link http://www.thingsiwishihadtaughtmyson.com/3/points.html

> *Just a few points,*
> *Your papi*

✉ **#15 THINGS I WISH I HAD TAUGHT MY SON... AND STILL CAN**
Storms of life...

Today the storm didn't arrive. We braced for a hurricane and instead got a sunny day. Not a drop of rain fell today.

But there will be storms in your life. There have been storms in your life already. On some of those, I couldn't shelter you. Sometimes some of your storms will be dark and ominous and feel endless and hopeless. But they will end and the sun will come out.

I just finished watching a movie with your sisters called *Bella,* an excellent movie that you too have seen. The first line in the movie is… "If you want to make God laugh, tell him your plans."

Just as I completed the last sentence above one of your little brothers came in with an acorn seed. He listened in awe as I pointed at the giant oak tree outside the window. This is the way the dialogue went.

"You see that big tree?," I said.

"Uh huh!"

"Well, that tree came from a seed like this."

"Hey Miguel… Come here…"

And then your brother ran out together and started immediately planting an acorn, talking about how big a tree it would become. And chances are high that the seed won't ever sprout. And that they'll forget that they ever planted it. But God is laughing.

I got a phone call that lasted about 15 minutes and guess what? Some storm clouds arrived during the call… Remnants of Hurricane Ike, I guess. This afternoon, the people of Galveston and Houston are picking up the pieces from the massive storm that arrived this morning. I know many prayed that it would be over and it is now. But some will have lost possessions, homes, pets, and loved ones. Their storms will continue beyond the winds and the rain.

When your storms arrive, you'll need to remember that they too will pass. No matter how severe it may seem, things will get better. Time will heal things. Somehow, you will grow from it all. And you will help others weather their storms.

> *It looks like drops are starting to fall now,*
> *Your papi*

✉ #16 THINGS I WISH I HAD TAUGHT MY SON... AND STILL CAN
Dime con quien andas...

There is a saying that I grew up with, a Spanish proverb that is quite wise. I heard it from my father, my mother and from other adults in my community. It was "Dime con quien andas y te diré quien eres." Here goes the translation: Tell me (show me) who your friends are and I will tell you who you are.

I know your friends up to this point in your life. I know they have been good friends. I am grateful to them for being good friends to my son. They have kept you out of trouble over the years and do genuinely care about you. Some of them, you'll have for life and grow old with.

Many of the friends people meet along the path of life are friends met in school, church, organizations and work. Later in life, some friendships form around children and the parents of their friends. Life will take you places and upon arrival, you will be introduced to lasting friends, temporary friends, mere acquaintances, friends who will change your life for the better or the worse, friends who will love you unconditionally, friends who will have a price tag, friends who will be shallow, friends who will be willing to die for you.

So whom will you hang out with? That is the term you use!

You see, hangin' will determine who you will become at certain stages in your life. Who you turn out to be will literally hang on whom you decide to hang with. That's the gist of the proverb, "Dime con quien andas y te diré quien eres."

Today you asked me if I would object to your considering a Greek fraternity. You said you would meet people, cool people. And we briefly spoke about the other less desirable attributes of a college fraternity. Still, this is your life and these are your decisions. Just remember that every thing is connected to everything. And hang wisely.

> *Now go and hang out,*
> *Your papi*

PS: I am a part of several fraternities, none of them Greek. I do however see the value of a brotherhood, and how a positive influence it can be. I cannot see you 24/7 nor choose your friends for you, but when I do get to meet your friends from your fraternity or otherwise, I'll remind you of that saying that I've heard throughout my life... Dime con quien andas y te diré quien eres.

#17 THINGS I WISH I HAD TAUGHT MY SON... AND STILL CAN
The hunt for gold October...

I once went on a photo shoot to the state of Jalisco in Mexico and travelled with a wonderful photographer who was in a teaching mood. We had to photograph the beauty and industry of Jalisco for that state's investment board. On that trip I learned a nice lesson that I remembered this morning.

As my dad and I drove to school to drop off your little brothers and sister, I couldn't help noticing the golden beauty light that was bathing the same mundane buildings and houses I see every day. This morning the sun's rays were silky. The tire repair shop on the way to school looked like a piece of high art. The houses on the top of Inspiration Hill looked like a movie scene shot in the hills of Malibu, California.

What did I learn from the photographer in Jalisco? I learned that late September and the month of October are great for photography because the sun rises slower, softer and in a beauty-light slant. In other words, it illuminates everything with a softer golden light at dawn and at dusk. And I learned that this dawn and dusk light seems to linger a little longer. And that cameras really love it.

I know you're not into photography that much, at least not yet. But there is a vast amount to learn about the art of photography if you want to take nice pictures almost every time you get behind the lens. While modern day cameras will take a lot of the guesswork out of it for you, the stop-you-in-your-tracks pictures will often require that you to go "unplugged" sometimes. How you frame a picture... What you leave in, what you leave out will also help you tell a poetic story. But framing is a lesson for another day.

Even if you're not going to take a picture at dusk or dawn in October, just snap your own imaginary pictures as you stroll back to your dorm. And keep them in your mental photo album.

> *Click,*
> *Your papi*

#18 THINGS I WISH I HAD TAUGHT MY SON... AND STILL CAN
Where are you going?

There are many metaphors for life... A bowl of cherries, a box of chocolates (thanks Forrest), a game, a dream sequence, a roller-coaster ride, a flash, a movie... But the most common theme is the journey or the voyage.

So let's entertain that idea for the sake of this lesson.

If life is a journey and if you're on your way, then where is it that you're headed full speed ahead? Do you know? Do you know how to find out? Today's lesson is about how to find out where your life is going.

Fasten your seat belt…

About 25 years ago, I heard the following three questions and they impacted me. These three questions had the capacity to pierce the masks that I was hiding behind. These three questions had the power to make me stop and reflect on the "where" I was going. They centered me. I love these three questions.

You should consider asking yourself these three questions and answering them humbly and truthfully as you go through life. What are these three questions?

Brace yourself…

Take a deep breath.

OK… Here they are.

WHERE DOES YOUR FREE TIME GO? Yep… You have as much time as anybody else. Are you using your time wisely? Do you like what you're doing with your free time? Are you satisfied with what you accomplished today? Or would you have regrets if today were your last day?

WHERE ARE YOU THOUGHTS? That's right… Only you know what you dwell on, reflect on, and aspire to. No one else will ever know what thoughts are firing away in your brain synapses. Are there blanks of time that you have no accounting for? Is there a massive three ring circus of imagination in your mind right now? Are your thoughts inspiring you to grander things? The bottom line is… What in the world are you thinking about as you go through this chapter of your life?

Finally, the third question…

WHERE DOES YOUR MONEY GO? When you come into money, how do you spend it? Is it purely for today's entertainment? For the good times? Are you squirreling it away for some future dream business venture or entrepreneurial itch that you can't fully scratch yet? Are you wearing it? Eating it? Drinking it? Investing it? Losing it in the wash? Or under the car seat?

When you answer the above three questions, you'll know where you're headed at full throttle. You may say you are headed in a different direction but the true answers to these questions will be the "actual" direction your life is headed. You may not like where you're going. It may be dead-end. But at least you'll know.

And most importantly (and never forget this), if you don't like where that road leads, you can change directions.

Of course it would be much easier if we subscribed to Forrest Gump's box of chocolates metaphor (you never know what you're gonna get). But then again, that would be too easy.

> *So, I'll see you on the road of life,*
> *Your papi*

 #19 THINGS I WISH I HAD TAUGHT MY SON... AND STILL CAN
You know when you're "in" it...

Your sister's fifth game, the tie-breaker volleyball game that would decide who would walk out of the packed college gym crying with tears of happiness or with tears of pain began at 10:30 last night. It was loud. It was intense. The newspaper was there. It was a showdown.

Neither team wanted to lose. Both teams played like they would never get another chance to settle the score again.

You've heard of "the zone". It's that mythical and mystical place during a performance, a test, a game, a creative project. It is that "pattern recognition" moment where all the pieces of the puzzle fit. It is that ethereal space where time and biology are defied, gravity is ignored and all the remaining forces of nature are all collaborating with you. The "zone" looks like that scene in *The Matrix* where Neo is able to dodge the bullet. And most of the time when you're in the zone, you don't remember the specifics of how you did what you did.

Well... Your sister was in "the zone" last night.

She walked out onto the court with an Olympian confidence. She was masterfully intuiting where she needed to be in millisecond time frames. Her libero blue shirt in the midst of her white-shirted team was everywhere. As a libero (Wikipedia defines this as a player specialized in defensive skills in volleyball), your sister became one with the floor.

She stretched, jumped, contorted, dove, flipped, and rolled in order to dig, slam, set, bump, dink, pancake, hit, kill, power tip and jump serve. I don't usually yell at a game, you know that. But I couldn't contain myself. I was so amazed.

We had to stay up until about 1:30 in the morning rewinding the video of some of those gravity-defying things that she did. We also had to do it to lessen the pain. This morning, even though her team had less points at the end of the fifth game, her picture was on the cover of the sport's page with the headline, *"Digging it."* Like I said, it was intense, 31-29, 15-25, 25-22, 22-25, 15-13 was the final score on the board.

About "the zone"... You know what the zone feels like in a basketball context. You know what if feels like to have the universe conspire with you to make a leather ball go through a hoop 24 feet away while a 6' 5" tall defender is hovering above you and the opposing team is hissing at you.

The lesson for today is that "the zone" can be experienced in many different contexts throughout your life. As I stated before in the "presentation" email a few days ago, when you're at the height of preparedness and confidence you can do great things. Sometimes it takes countless mindless repetition and practice to arrive at the zone. Sometimes it requires allowing your intuition to run its course, uninterrupted. But that's a lesson for another day.

Now... Being "in the zone" and "zoning out" are two very different things. Strive for the first one in everything you do.

And call or text your sister... That's what big brothers are for.

To see one of her "in the zone" astonishing points, go to http://www.thingsiwishihadtaughtmyson.com/Dig/this.html

Don't mind your mami screaming in the background.

> *Until tomorrow,*
> *Your papi*

 #20 THINGS I WISH I HAD TAUGHT MY SON... AND STILL CAN
Happiness is... Part 1.

Ah, the eternal search for happiness. At some point, that becomes the obsession in life, to find happiness. According to the *Declaration of Independence* it is your unalienable right to have Life, Liberty and the Pursuit of Happiness.

And I guess that happiness in Thomas Jefferson's context revolves around making money. Perhaps that is why the concept of happiness has been hijacked by luxury cars, HD plasma screens, exclusive country clubs, high European fashion, exotic gastronomical experiences, ostentatious homes and synthetic body parts. And yet, I know many unhappy millionaires personally.

So what is happiness and how do you find it? And how do you keep it?

Of course, I only have my humble perspective. And I have met a great many people from all walks of life... Dirt poor to outrageously wealthy. Extremely healthy and fit to broken-hearted and terminally ill. And since this is about my transference of wisdom and perspective to you, I can offer this with a sense of confidence that I am right about this or at least very close to right.

This lesson is about how to attain happiness.

And I'm afraid that it will be a little counter-intuitive and extremely counter-cultural.

Here it goes... To become happy, to finally get to that elusive destination of true and lasting happiness, you'll have to give of yourself to others. You'll have to help make others happy without conditions. You'll have to free yourself from the self-love of your own ego.

There is profound truth in "it is better to give than to receive." Often, your time, intelligence and talents will be the "what" you give and in very few cases, giving money will be the right solution.

Just like in that fabulous movie *Pay it Forward*, you may never know who you affected with your influence and generosity because the effects will be several layers down and thousands of miles away, perhaps even across the globe. That's the cool part... The "not knowing" part.

But when you go to bed at night, right before you close your eyes, you won't wonder whether you've found happiness. You'll know.

> *Happy to be your father,*
> *Your papi*

✉ **#21 THINGS I WISH I HAD TAUGHT MY SON... AND STILL CAN**
The dreamer...

Mijo... You've probably already figured out that I'm a dreamer. I'm constantly chasing after grandiose dreams. Sometimes, I'm chasing my tail. Sometimes I wake up too early and don't remember how to finish the dream. Sometimes I don't follow up on some of the dreams because I have too much going on. But dreamin' stuff into reality is what I do.

Over the course of the last 20 years, I've had about 20 failed businesses and a few successful ones. In 1998, I tried to devise a product like Peerflix for people to swap CDs. I didn't have the right technology to implement. The idea was right. The timing was off. In 2001 I proposed gobedo.com to the Centers for Disease Control to help end the obesity problem in this country. The GOBEDO program was a web portal that rewarded kids for exercising and doing outdoorsy things. The CDC didn't buy it. Obesity is still one of the largest threats to coach-potato children today. Was I crazy to propose this back then? Today there are a few corporations trying to implement this kind of idea, albeit on a smaller scale.

Obviously, the successful businesses and dreams I have pursued in the past have taken care of our family 'til now. But when your mom and I first got married we instantly sank into debt. We suffered two miscarriages leaving us demoralized and 12K in debt. I also had my college loan to pay for and mami was going to school. With more babies and private school costs came an out-of-control spiraling into even deeper debt that would require bigger ideas and bigger dreams. Thank God they came.

Our family eventually had a chance to come up for air about 10 years ago, but my entrepreneurial itch has kept us precariously teetering on the edge of bankruptcy. Our biggest expense however is not our home or our vehicles... It's the educational and character-building guidance we seek for our children followed by our investment in technology, intellectual property and business development tools. While this "dreaming" may sound irresponsible at face value, I assure you that I consider my family's short and long-term needs before anything else.

My job (or love) for the last five years is a 24-hour job. Even during sleep do I ideate. I do what I like. Lately, I've been feeling myself entering "the zone". I am averaging one new invention or business idea (or enhancement to a company I already have) per week. My dreams are in HD now. When Paul Goya (The Brand Equator) and I embarked on writing *The Olé Degree,* we had no idea that we would be taken on the most incredible ride of our lives. More importantly, the book helped us to arrive at a very long and forgotten approach to business-building, one rooted in the principles of persuasion and in the art of brand framing. I'll let you know about these in later emails.

For now, know that all these past semi-successful dreams have been dress rehearsals for the bigger dreams that are around the corner. Of course, some will stay on my mental shelf and collect mental dust indefinitely. But save this email because I can see into the future. And in that future, some of these ideas will stick… Grow from infancy into important enterprises. And when I pinch myself, I'll be awake.

The lesson for today is to dream.

Dream on,
Your papi

 #22 THINGS I WISH I HAD TAUGHT MY SON… AND STILL CAN
Be there… All there.

Life is a series of conversations, some mundane, some life-altering. In the life-altering department, the problem is you never know when you're going to be the one whose life will be empowered or robbed by the conversation… Or the one who, through your words and attention, will do the empowering or the damage to the other person. Ideally, it will be positive and reciprocal.

There are thousands of distractions in a single day, all vying for your attention: Ads, homework, hunger pangs, texts, emails, calls, TV shows, internet sites, mental lists, countless to-dos, background music, girls, friends, etc…

The lesson today is around what to do when you are engaged in a conversation with someone, anyone… Friend, teacher, parent, sibling, cashier, study partner, RA, roommate, etc…

The lesson for today is that if and when you are conversing with someone, be totally there. Listen intently. Be able to repeat back the specifics of the transference of information that the other person is conveying to you. Often we can get into an uh hum, uh hum, uh hum groove in an effort to pretend that we are listening when, in fact, we're off in a distant galactic loop.

Even your quietest of friends will want to be listened to when they speak. Even your never-serious jokester friends will want your undivided attention. And as long as you're going to be taking part in that conversation, might as well make the complete investment in that person. Texting, typing an email or searching the Internet while conversing will probably bring an abrupt end to the conversation.

Uh hum, uh hum, uh hum… Won't cut it.

As I stated above, your divided attention has the power to alter somebody's life negatively because he or she may withdraw from an important conversation, all because your inattention turned him or her off. Or perhaps someday when you "really" need to talk to a friend (one of those lay-it-on-the-line talks), they may reciprocate your shallow, attention-deficit behavior… And you'll turn off.

If you want to have insurance against this happening to you, simply be there to listen when you're needed. Be focused. Be awake. Be aware. Be supportive. Be a friend.

When you get an incoming text while engaged in a conversation. Consider ignoring it. That will be a clear and important gesture to the person opposite of you that he or she is being honored.

> *Whenever you want to talk, I'll be there,*
> *Your papi*

PS: You little brother just came and announced that he can now make the big puzzles like the big boys. Perhaps it gave me an opportunity to learn from this lesson too. All I did was look into his big bright happy eyes as he proudly explained the details of the Pterodactyl puzzle he's building. That's all it took to make a difference in his life.

 #23 THINGS I WISH I HAD TAUGHT MY SON… AND STILL CAN
It's a tradition around here…

This morning, your little brother was wearing a shirt that you wore. And that your next oldest brother wore. And that your second oldest brother wore. You know the shirt. It's the striped Snoopy shirt. It's finally starting to come undone a little in the shoulder area and the screen print is cracked and fading. But hey… It's tradition.

And the value of tradition is the lesson for today.

As a family, we have several traditions. Since you were one month old, we celebrated Easter a certain way. That tradition is one that has gone back at least 50 years. It connects you and I to a piece of history. Some traditions that we have mami or I have instituted for our immediate family. Others are traditions that have been adopted from our church, the schools you attended or the organizations we belong to.

For the last three years or so, I have taken my father out to breakfast to share nopalitos and life. It has been a beautiful tradition. You and I often spoke about the search for the perfect ham, egg and cheese taco when you were an early teen. We visited many different taquerias in search of the elusive be-all and end-all breakfast taco. I guess this tacological pursuit constitutes a long-standing tradition in your life. And I believe that to this day, this combination is still the preferred taco mash-up you regularly order.

What other traditions will you establish in your life, in your family's life? What traditions will the big brother of the family propose to his younger siblings? Will it revolve around a video game, a yearly Madden Football challenge? Will the Eagle Scout go out on a hike with his Boy Scout, and Cub Scout brothers?

When I was a kid, my father and uncle usually made a "carne asada" cookout in the backyard. It was the highlight of our Sunday afternoon. I'm not the accomplished BBQ-ing pro that they were but perhaps it is a good idea to consider a tradition like this.

Believe it or not, saying "I love you" was not a tradition in our family. Of course, it was understood that we were loved, but the words "I love you" we not the norm. Now we have a tradition in our family of saying "I love you". Now my father says it regularly, sparingly. And when we spoke this morning about all the stuff that is going on at school, writing assignments, reading assignments and so forth… Right before you hit "end call" on your cell phone, you said three very powerful and important words to me that sent chills up my spine. You said, "I love you."

> *I love you too,*
> *Your papi*

PS: As a gesture of solidarity with your tradition, I will eat a ham, egg and cheese taco tomorrow.

 #24 THINGS I WISH I HAD TAUGHT MY SON… AND STILL CAN D G and A…

Your guitar is gathering dust. The magical instrument that came free with the purchase of your drums is sitting lonely in your mom's closet. Yet the guitar is a great college buddy. I remember learning how to play the guitar between reading assignments, writing assignments, design assignments and the tedious reviewing for tests during long nights.

I didn't consider playing the guitar until I was a sophomore in college. My girlfriend played the guitar and at my insistence she taught me a few chords, D, G and A on her guitar.

Feeling the desire to learn the guitar beyond these few chords, I went to Nuevo Laredo to buy a classical guitar and to the music store to buy a chord book.

I found that if I knew how to sing a song already and had the chords in front of me I could learn at a faster clip. So I concentrated on church songs because I knew how to sing them. And then I embarked on writing songs for my girlfriend. Somewhere, on some shelf in our house, is a cassette tape with some of those humble songs.

The lesson for today is to master the chords D, G and A.

You can play hundreds of songs with just these three chords. *Hey there Delilah* is one of them (sort of).

I remember studying at our apartment dining room table when at the University of Texas at Austin. Next to the table was my guitar, a sort of reward between my self designated accomplishments. Read a chapter, play the guitar. Wash the clothes, play the guitar. My cousin Oscar, my roommate at the time, made fun of my songwriting. I guess some of those songs were rather silly and perhaps a little mushy. But hey, they worked. She married me.

With D, G and A, you can play the Barney song (I love you, you love me… That song that you used to love), the ABCs song, the Happy Birthday song or *Las Mañinitas* (the Spanish version). You can play the Beatles *Get Back* or *Love Me Do* or John Mellencamp's *Jack & Diane… Free-Fallin'* can be played with these chords too. You can jam to *La Bamba* or any ranchera that you hear blaring out of taqueria jukeboxes.

So when you come home next time, consider taking the guitar with you. Get those three chords down and you'll be on your way to a lifetime of instant concerts in your own room.

> *Strummin' out,*
> *Your papi*

 #25 THINGS I WISH I HAD TAUGHT MY SON… AND STILL CAN
What will your "life work" be?

Your life is like on giant Google search mode. You are looking for what you want to be, what you want to do. You're asking questions, absorbing answers and wondering.

Well, I've got something for you to consider. Don't find the "life work" that makes you money. Find the "life work" that makes your life more satisfying even if it pays peanuts. If it pays well, great.

I'm not proposing that you live in poverty. No… I'm suggesting you follow the career that excites you and find out how to make money through some other means. I will be teaching you some of those other means in these emails. While some of these "ways" to make money will require great effort in the beginning they will not demand much effort later, allowing you to explore life to the fullest.

I read *The 4-Hour Work Week* a few months ago. That's right! 4 hours a week. A crazy book! An insightful book. The writer details how he gallivants around the world doing what he wants to do, not what he has to do while making the necessary money to be happy. Obviously, writing a popular book adds to that livelihood, but he was "living" his chosen life before the book.

I am on a race to create and market intellectual property so that I don't have to work for a typical boss or client the rest of my life. I am also doing it because I'm not invincible and our large family will need support if I am not available to provide physically for that support.

Intellectual property can come in the form of books, movies, TV shows, t-shirts, TV networks, composed music, lyrics, brands, photography, videos, video footage, inventions, websites, web portals, witty sayings, greeting cards, how-to's for video game cheat codes, instruction manuals for being a successful college student, exotic sound effects, etc…

I am trying my hand at many of these. Some will stick… Some will bomb. But I will have a rich memory of having tried lots of things…

As for you… Once you find your true calling, there will be an opportunity to create an intellectual property product or products around that love. And others will be happy to be your customers if you do it well.

> Live,
> Your papi

 #26 THINGS I WISH I HAD TAUGHT MY SON… AND STILL CAN
Between a wall and a hard place…

I don't know if your professors are talking about this… But there is a gigantic problem in the world right now. It has been caused by a shell game of deceit. A term that you will hear for years to come is "mortgage-backed securities". It'll be in future history books. It'll cripple the next presidency. And this one will affect you if it hasn't already done so.

Imagine a giant domino maze, and the first domino is Wall Street and somewhere in the middle is the domino that represents you. Further down the domino effect are the people in Gary, Indiana, or Mobile, Alabama, or San Antonio who will get laid off, and ultimately it'll reach Bangladesh.

There, women who gets loans in increments of $7 or $8 a month to buy the supplies they need to make one handmade chair per day with the intent to sell, will not get that money. They will probably go hungry, lose strength and perhaps never regain the ability to make another chair. And then die. And so will their children.

Because of outright runaway greed and sheer disregard for the rest of humanity, the highest levels of commerce and the highest levels of government have betrayed not only us, but also the entire world.

Once on a trip to New York (the day after the bombing of the underground parking garage of the World Trade Center), I fell for an actual, in-the-flesh "shell game". It's probably the oldest scam in the world. I was walking around in Lower Manhattan because I had been producing some music for a TV commercial in a tiny cellar studio and wanted to get a breath of fresh (sort of fresh) air. I was with a friend of mine named Rafael. I had $60 in my wallet for my trip.

So we come upon a little makeshift table where it seems that a stupid guy is losing money, $20 after $20 after $20. And I think to myself, "Man this guy is stupid." That's because I knew where the ball was. I could follow it as the shells were being shuffled. The "stupid" guy was getting it wrong most of the time and losing hundreds of dollars. Then the shuffler turns to me and sees that I'm engaged in what is going on. "Hey, you think you know where the ball is?" I try to ignore him but he's in my face. I think I eventually nod yes.

"You sure?"

I say, "Yes."

"You got $20?"

I don't respond.

"C'mon let me just see it."

And like an idiot, I show him that I have $20.

As I show it to him, he grabs it and says something like, "OK Hot Shot, where do you think the ball is?" Everybody is watching. I'm confused as hell and my pride has kicked in. But I know where the ball is, right?

I point to where I last saw the ball. He raises the shell (actually I think it was a plastic cup), and it wasn't there. I turn red with embarrassment, and Rafael is quite afraid about the whole ordeal. I turn around and can't believe what is going on. Here I am on a back street just south of Chinatown playing a shell game. How did this happen? The shuffler sees that I'm upset and says something like, "Hey don't worry about it." The remaining two cups are still down. "You can win it back easy. Just put another $20 down. And tell me where it is."

I don't quite remember how he got my other $20. I think somebody whispers to me that the ball is under the right cup. It's a blur. I guess wrong again and lose $40 total. I have $20 left and another day in New York.

What I didn't know was that my senses didn't fool me. What I didn't know was that there were three guys involved in this scam. I thought that there was only one, the shuffler. The "stupid" guy losing the $20 after $20 was part of the scam. And the guy standing just off to the side of the table was removing the ball from under the cup while the very confident, in-your-face shuffler was distracting me. Everybody watching knew what was going on? And nobody stopped it. They just watched one more sucker get robbed.

I wanted so much to tell the next victim that it was a scam, but I found out later that these guys were quite capable of stabbing anybody or me who threatened their enterprise.

These guys took $40 bucks from me in 1993, but today, the guys on Wall Street will probably end up taking several trillion dollars from people that work at Walmart or who toil in factories across America. They will be the reason you may never get a student loan. They will be the reason why after 20 years of setting aside money from a very squeezed paycheck, fully half of the savings our family had counted on will disappear, perhaps never to be replaced. Their shell game will involve having coordinated carefully with Senators and members Congress (from both parties) to be the be guys who move the cup, act as if they are the ones losing (the $20), or are the accomplice bystanders who know that the behavior of the "shuffling shell guys" is immoral, rotten to the core of humanity but legal.

What is being debated tonight in Washington is whether we should feel pity towards the "shell game guys" and find it in our hearts to send them an extra 700 billion dollars so that they can get a new table, new shells and a new ball so that they can continue to legally flush what's left of our livelihood down the toilet of misery. Certainly, the president just came on the tube a few hours ago to tell us that he wants us to write a blank check to buy the cancer of the financial world so that the very same gambling addicts can go out and place new high risk wagers. And the whole thing will be framed as a necessary evil to rebound the country. And in three or four months, we'll be right back in the same spot when all the credit card companies collapse and want a bail-out too.

The lesson for today is… Beware of the shell game. In all its forms.

Bailing out now,
Your papi

"Life is not measured by the breaths we take, but by the moments that take our breath away." — *Unknown Author*

 #27 THINGS I WISH I HAD TAUGHT MY SON… AND STILL CAN
Respect other people's beliefs…

Not every person believes what you believe. Not every person has a large family. Not every person has enjoyed good health. Not every person has lived in a safe neighborhood. Not every person is from Texas. Not every person speaks English. Not every person acknowledges a God. Not every person likes cynical comedy. And although it is hard to believe… Not everybody loves tortillas.

In college, the world converges and you immerse yourself in intertwined cultures. Some are fascinating, desirable, cool. Some are mysterious to you, awkward and illogical. To them, you may be just as different, and quite strange.

Most people rush to judgment without even considering the context of the people they are judging. It's a convenient but lazy thing to do. The human mind compresses all the information it absorbs and packs it into little mental boxes that make sense. The brain does this to function properly. These mental boxes are called stereotypes. And yes, everybody stereotypes others because the brain doesn't want to overheat with overload. It is quite impossible to go through life without stereotyping. Much to people's surprise, stereotyping isn't inherently bad. What usually causes problems and negative consequences for all is stereotyping with old or wrong information. The good news is that negative stereotyping can be avoided with genuine interest and meaningful and sensitive dialogue. Resist the urge to categorize, generalize.

Perhaps someday, if you haven't already experienced it, you may stumble onto a well-intentioned person with a good heart but with a myopic perspective of other people. He may impose the value system he feels is the only value system that matters. People in cultural training wheels may be extremely passionate about their cause, their view. Respect it. Take it in from different angles. Try to understand their context (circumstances, conditions, factors, state of affairs, situation, background, setting, etc). If there is an opportunity to broaden the aperture of that point of view, great. If that moment is not the right moment, so be it. Just know that you will have another opportunity to grow the box, change the box, reshape the box. And that includes yours.

As a young man of Mexican heritage, others will either gracefully or rudely share with you their Mexican perception boxes (as learned from *Fools Rush In* or the Taco Bell Chihuahua dog). As a member of a family of eight, you'll hear all kinds of jokes where your mom and I are the butt of that joke. I've heard 'em all. Don't worry, we can take it. And you don't take it personally. We love our eight children. We love you.

> *Think outside of the box,*
> *Your papi*

 ### #28 THINGS I WISH I HAD TAUGHT MY SON... AND STILL CAN
Have you ever had a Vújà De?

There is a French word that we use in the United States when we get that awkward feeling that we've been there done that, only we've never been there, nor done that. It usually happens when you travel to some new city or new country. You feel like you've been there before. Déjà Vu is the word... Day ja voo is the way the word sounds. But that's not what this lesson is about.

No, this lesson is about something I have quite frequently. It's a Vújà De... Pronounced Voo Ja Day.

George Carlin, the comedian, is probably the first person to make this word known. I don't know how he used it, just that Tom Kelly, the author of *The Ten Faces of Innovation* mentions that Mr. Carlin joked about it in his stand-up routine. But Tom Kelly went on to describe this condition I had been having and that I experience now (probably two or three times a week). It started happening with great frequency during and after the writing of Paul's and my book. Tom Kelly mentioned that he and some of his colleagues had Vújà Des. I finally knew what I had. And perhaps you already have them too, but haven't noticed.

If a déjà vu is that feeling of seeing and sensing something familiar that you've never actually experienced, a Vújà De is the opposite. It is seeing something that has always been there, but that no others have seen.

For example, I believe the founder of Curves, the gym for women had a Vújà De at some point. He bought a fitness center in Houston, but the business venture collapsed. At some point, he and his exercise-enthusiast wife designed an fitness environment that was women-friendly (unlike the big gym meat markets walled with hundreds of mirrors).

The Vújà De this couple had was that they saw what nobody else had seen, or if they had seen it brushed it off as not valuable. They saw that millions of women were not comfortable with the Bally's and Gold's Gyms of the world yet wanted to keep fit. This little piece of Vújà De insight became a 2.6 billion dollar business. This little company that started in Harlingen, Texas, had 6,000 franchises within seven years and now has over 10,000 franchises in 60 countries. This little business became the world's largest fitness franchise.

You have Vújà Des too. Everybody does. But you may probably listen too much to that little voice in your head that says, "That's a stupid idea." I've permanently kicked that voice out of my head. It wasn't paying rent. That's why I'm doing such crazy things right now.

> *Go out and have a Vújà De day,*
> *Your papi*

 #29 THINGS I WISH I HAD TAUGHT MY SON... AND STILL CAN
Nothing like homemade...

Cafeteria food is great for a while... And then you miss your mom's Mexican rice.

At a certain point in your college experience, you start to value all those things you didn't like as much when you were at home. One of those things is the particular way mom made eggs in the morning. Another is her way of making stews, spaghetti and steaks. I still remember how food tasted in the house where I grew up.

When I left to Austin for college, my roommate knew how to cook. I could defend myself too. One of the practices he suggested we do was that we eat full course homemade meals in the evening when we returned to our apartment. This was done to reduce our "eating out" costs.

That's when I called my mom to ask her how she made rice, her signature rice, the rice I wouldn't eat when I was a kid, the same rice that was so unimportant growing up but which all of a sudden meant a sense of well-being in my college years.

"First you brown the rice. You pour about a cup of rice onto a skillet (I recommend a Teflon skillet as they are more forgiving) and add a little cooking oil, just enough to lightly coat the rice. You stir the rice around as the oil heats up. All you want to do is brown the rice, don't burn it. It doesn't take very long."

This was part of the conversation on the long distance call in the days when one minute cost about 40¢.

"Then you pour about three cups of water," the conversation continued (Usually, the water contacting the hot skillet creates a bundle of steam. Just be careful…).

It's been a while since I've personally made rice so I consulted with your mom for this. The styles of Mexican rice today are as varied as the genres of music today. But for that Mexican rice flavor that you grew accustomed to, one of the three cups of water is mixed in with some form of chicken bouillon cube. One brand that you can use is Knorr. This is dehydrated chicken stock (with lots of salt) that dissolves in boiling water making the mix into a chicken soup broth. Your mom uses something a little different though. She uses two products from Goya interchangeably. One is called Sazón Cilantro con Tomate and the other is called Sazón con Azafrán… Really tasty stuff.

So as my mother stated, you add the three cups of water, one of which is the dissolved bouillon or the other seasoning mom uses and bring the heat up on the mix of ingredients to a low boil. Then you reduce the heat and let it simmer for about 10 to 15 minutes. The water will be absorbed into the rice and it will plump-up with saffron, cilantro and chicken broth flavor (depending on the spice you use). Also, just before it's ready, my college roommate taught me to add a half can or a full can of tomato sauce (so that its consistency in the rice could be seen). Monitor that the rice isn't sticking to the bottom of the skillet as the water disappears. And taste test to make sure it's ready.

And then voilà!

You'll have homesick dorm neighbors coming from around to see what the magical smell is all about.

> Con sazón,
> Your papi

PS: Don't burn your tongue while taste-testing or your whole night and tomorrow's meals will be ruined.

✉ #30 THINGS I WISH I HAD TAUGHT MY SON... AND STILL CAN
Recipe for reciprocation.

I subscribe to something called the *Principle of Reciprocity*. I believe that when you help people, they'll usually help you when you are in need. When you were a young Scout, you helped other Scouts with their Eagle Scout project. When it was time to complete yours, several of the younger Scouts came to your aid. But they were also reciprocating your past deeds because they had experienced your leadership and support during their early Scout camp-outs. Others who came to help on your project (adults and family members) came because they were reciprocating favors or behaviors your mom and I had done beforehand for them. Still others came because they valued what your project meant for the school. They reciprocated through their appreciation.

In almost every culture around the world (if not all), this principle is perpetuated. According to Robert Cialdini, probably the most respected author on the subject of "Persuasion", he states that the *Principle of Reciprocity* sounds something like this: "I am obligated to give back to you the form of behavior that you first give to me." In other words, "I am willing and waiting to help you in any way that I can because you have helped me in some important or meaningful way already."

Throughout my life, I have been helped countless times by people who knew me and by total strangers too. I am truly grateful for the support I have received along the way. And I have tried to remember and give back. In the cases where I have not reciprocated the support I received, I am ready and willing to mirror the behavior. For some, I have already returned the gesture without having been asked. Then there are those who may be saving their "request" for when my particular expertise corresponds with the need they have. I look forward to helping in those cases too.

The *Principle of Reciprocity* works best when you are the one who first gives the helping hand, the boost, and the favor. And yes, you should do it unconditionally. Never should you feel like the other person is obligated to pay you back. Luckily for you and society, most people are already culturally wired that way. They want to give back. So that the cycle continues.

According to Cialdini, this principle works with things like service (lending a hand or talent, etc.), information (lessons, tips and shortcuts, etc.) and concessions (compromising when an impasse occurs).

When a community is healthy, there is so much giving back and forth that it all gets confusing. There is an abundance of love and hope and generosity. As I mentioned in a past email, listening on purpose to somebody when they need an ear is a form of showing you care. I get called all the time to lend an ear... And to listen non-judgmentally.

One final suggestion from Cialdini is that we learn to accept somebody's gratitude too. Gratitude is like the glue of a society of givers. Perhaps we may sometimes be too proud to accept help. Accept it. Sometimes we may be too quick to say "no thank you". Instead, say thank you for helping. And sometimes when we've done a good deed, we may sometimes say, "Awe, it was nothing" or "don't mention it." Next time you help somebody through a rough spot or help somebody succeed at something, and he or she turns to thank you for the help, consider saying the following, "I know you'd probably do the same for me if the situation were reversed."

And the world will continue to spin happily.

> *Reciprocate with a smile,*
> *Your papi*

 #31 THINGS I WISH I HAD TAUGHT MY SON... AND STILL CAN
Take pictures... Because they'll take you back.

One of our biggest family treasures today is that both your mom and I had decent cameras, and we loved to take pictures. We literally have thousands of paper pictures of you guys doing every conceivable "first".

You are growing up in a MySpace and Facebook age, where everybody posts pictures of everyday stuff. Make sure you keep copies of those in an organized fashion. You're fortunate to be living in a digital era where the cost of snapping a picture isn't averaging to $14 a roll (that's what it cost for us to shoot about 36 pictures). Today, it's just a little extra space on the hard drive or on a CD-ROM. And they're email-able.

I understand that nanotubes are coming too. These are portable storage devices that hold about 700 gigs. One of these storage devices could hold all the pictures we've ever snapped. Regardless of the format, you have a unique opportunity to capture all the special moments of your life. Even your phone has a camera. And it goes with you everywhere. Your phone camera is okay for outdoor shots, but when you earn some money, you may want to consider a better camera, even a used one.

The lesson for today is to snap away. Take pictures of special things, mundane things, anything. Learn to label your pictures so they all don't say DSCN and a number. If you don't heed this warning, you may find yourself writing (erasing) over some important pictures because the same name from a different camera was imported onto your computer, replacing your friend's wedding portrait with a picture of a college buddy picking his nose.

When you take pictures, look for interesting framing. What you leave out of the framing of a picture can make what you leave in infinitely more interesting. Angles are always nice because they present for us views of life that we don't normally see. I have always used cameras with swivel view screens so that I can shoot up without having to be lying on the floor and shoot down without being on a ladder.

Light is tricky, and it will take a lifetime to understand it well. And you'll feel very empowered as you learn to mold it. I do. Yesterday morning your little brother went out into the October golden morning sun that I mentioned a few emails back. I kicked myself for having left the camera at work. I had to take a mental picture, instead. You'll have to believe me. It was breath-taking.

One last note… Your mom and I didn't have the instant capacity to see the pictures we took (on the spot) like digital cameras allow us to do so now. However, what instantaneity has adversely done is given you the power to delete the bad pictures. The blurry pictures. The dark pictures. The stupid gesture pictures. We have some horrible pictures stored away in many shoeboxes. Guess what? Some of those are the special ones now. Those are the real ones, not the fakey posed ones. So my advice to you is don't erase all your blurry, fuzzy, imperfect pictures. Perhaps they'll be able to take you back to a more real reality.

> *Snapping away now,*
> *Your papi*

 #32 THINGS I WISH I HAD TAUGHT MY SON… AND STILL CAN
Laugh out loud… Really loud!!!

I've never heard you laugh loud… Uncontrollably… Without abandon. I've never seen you spray out your soda because something funny caught you off guard. I've never seen you get the laugh hiccups, nor ha-ha hyperventilate, nor slap your thighs in stupid-looking contortions because you couldn't stop laughing. What's up with that?

OK… So I heard you laughing out loud when we went to watch *Napoleon Dynamite* together. That was probably the most I've ever heard you laugh.

I mentioned a few emails ago that there are Vújà Des waiting to be found all around us. In Mumbai, India, Dr. Madan Kataria decided that he was going to start a movement. Perhaps he had a Vújà De. By pursuing the funny hypothesis tickling him he probably saved countless lives. I'm sure he has enhanced the quality of life of millions of people, too. He organized hundreds of Indian citizens in a park and showed them how to gain better fitness, take deeper breaths, limber up and flex their body. How he did it was novel.

I laugh a lot. I laugh out loud at the radio when something surprisingly funny happens. I laugh at work because I plan to laugh. I spend my day trying to be funny with a co-worker who reciprocates. Your ex-coach laughs a lot, too. He slaps his hands, his head, his lap… He knows the value of a good laugh.

That's what Dr. Kataria does. He laughs out loud. He teaches random people in the park to force their laugh while exercising their bodies until the forced laughs are so incredibly silly and stupid-looking that a natural laugh arrives, causing laugh contagion. And contagion is the appropriate word because this laughter has spread across the world. Today you can either join one of The Laughter Clubs in Austin, Houston or San Antonio. There is not one presently in your college town. But they are everywhere. And to think we missed National Laughter day on May 6.

I've sent an email to the coordinator of the Laughter Club here and perhaps I will go to witness firsthand, what it feels like to laugh without purpose… To look utterly stupid. Your mom thinks that it's just silly. I say, "That's the point."

> *Getting the last laugh… LOL,*
> *Your papi*

 #33 THINGS I WISH I HAD TAUGHT MY SON… AND STILL CAN
Celebrate life… Even in death.

Today is my mother's birthday… She would have been 81. October 2nd is always a day of reflection for me. Plus, my good friend Steve always reminds me days in advance that mami's birthday is coming soon. My dad and I talked about her at breakfast and the rest of the day wandering whispers of memories arrived of her.

When she was winding down, during her chemo treatments for the cancer that had spread throughout her lymph system, we used to visit her on weekends. During this time, I was working all week in Chicago and would arrive in San Antonio, grab the family and head for Corpus. She was quite uncomfortable. Two things that I did to send her off with fond memories was that I took my guitar to the hospice. I took my church song music book and sang to her all her oldies but goodies. Nurses would come in and out. I don't know if they had that type of guest before. But I know she enjoyed it even though it was hard for her to communicate.

Another thing that I did (this was the year 2000) was that I let her see the picture show I created for her funeral. I scanned about a 100 pictures. Ordered them. Set them to music. I remember holding the laptop above her bed pointing it down so that she could see the celebration of her life that the picture show would be. Through a series of blinks and low moans, she was able to tell me that I had a picture of some total stranger in my slide show (I thought it was her). That was a peaceful humorous moment.

My mami had a very strong will. I guess I have inherited some of that dogged persistence from her. I guess you'll get some of it from me. But I would like to add that my mom was a rule breaker. While raising six kids she sought an education. For many years she pursued a master's degree. As a kid I found myself roaming college libraries while mami was in class. Once when I was about 12, my grandmother, my mom and I took a Greyhound bus trip to Warner Robbins, Georgia, just south of Macon, just south of Atlanta. I have a very vivid and beautiful snapshot in my mind of the details of this trip.

My mami loved to sing. She loved to eat… She loved her tortillas semi-burned. She loved impromptu massages. She loved her novelas. She loved to read. She loved being a first grade teacher. She loved her children. She loved her naps. She wanted to hang on to meet the last of her grandchildren. She made me promise that I wouldn't have more when our sixth was born. But I guess God pulled rank and sent two more blessings. I'm sure she is happy for us.

Last Thursday, our former pastor visited the church for a memorial service for Alejandro, a friend of mine. He spoke about a specific Psalm, his favorite. It goes like this… "In the sight of the angels O Lord, I will sing your praise, I will sing your praise." As you know his mother too passed away a few years ago. Well, he comforted Alejandro and said his mother; my mami and his (the pastor's) mother were all in heaven singing in the "sight of the angels". And they were having a celebration.

My mom is the closest person to me that has ever moved on. Writing about her now has triggered a flood of fond memories. Funny, all the not-so-fond memories have dissolved away.

Someday someone close to you will move on to that eternal part of life that we are meant for. It will be painful, but find the beauty in it. Make sure you celebrate the life of that person if you find yourself in the role of having to say a few words. As you know, I'm in a business where I share life with people who are focused on getting their stories documented for future generations. Some are terminal. Some have decades more to explore life. Some just want to look good for their grandkids and have done it well in advance. All have come to the realization that they won't live forever.

The lesson for today is to not fear death. It is a part of life, eternal life. And when someone close to you is gone physically, that doesn't mean that you don't remember him or her on their days of celebration.

> *Happy birthday mami,*
> *Your papi*

PS: I know you have a lot to read, but when you get a breather. *The Last Lecture* by Randy Pausch is a life-changing book.

✉ **#34 THINGS I WISH I HAD TAUGHT MY SON... AND STILL CAN**
Are you BPMing?

Last weekend, your third oldest sister brought home a Guinea pig, the classroom pet. Its name was Buddy. It was a bit nervous but quite gentle. Obviously, we kept the cats away. Buddy went back on Monday in one piece. All was well.

The Guinea pig is not a pig. It's not from Guinea either. They belong to the Cavidae family. They are from the Andes of South America. If I remember correctly, they are a food item in some parts of South America. They are very docile which is why they have served as great pets in the United States. They were brought by European traders in the 16th century. Because they were used for scientific experimentation in the early 1900s (they were seen as perfect organisms for the use of science), the term Guinea pig became a metaphor in English for being the subject of experimentation.

This weekend, I felt like a pig, A Guinea pig. Your second oldest sister is working on her science project, and I am her test subject. She has me doing sit-ups, push-ups (I can barely do them), running a mile, checking for my flexibility, checking for my strength capacity, checking my resting heart rate, my max heart rate, etc… She's got me sweating and grunting like a pig.

I've been reading lots of books about aging and slowing its effects. I thought I was doing it for my father, to help him get a few more innings out of his game. But I realized quickly that at 43, this was the time that I also needed to consider my bout with the aging process. Two of the most important books I read was *You, The Instruction Manual* and *Younger Next Year*. Of course they talked about the need for a healthy diet, but I recommend the book *Super Foods* for that. The lesson I wanted to pass on to you is the lesson of resting heart rate and max heart rate.

Before reading these two books that I mentioned first, I had seen people with heart rate monitors, but I had no clue what they were for or how they worked. These two books spoke about them with great accuracy. Both were pretty forceful in their recommendation that to slow down the decaying of the body because of the aging process, a person must exercise at 60% his heart rate at least four times a week and at 80% his heart rate at least twice a week (Each workout should last an hour). The former is for burning fat. The latter is for developing new cell structure. During the reading of these books, I had another Vújà De (I saw something that had always been there). I realized that the language of the heart and the language of music are the same language. Let me explain. The rhythm of music is measured in BPM "beats per minute". Our pulse is measured in BPM "beats per minute". And because I was in the marching band in high school, I understood the concept of synchronizing movement to beats. I put all three together and decided to embark on making a product I call Heartbeatz Music which people can use to synchronize with in order to achieve a 60% and an 80% max heart rate without having to do all the complicated math and formulas. Free samples of this music can be downloaded at http://www.heartbeatzmusic.com in exchange for feedback on how well the music worked in your cardio exercise routine. Let your friends know about it.

Heart rate = ((Max HR-Resting HR)*%X/100)+Resting HR (where %X =%MAX, e.g. 60). If you're interested in seeing the formula and how it works, visit www.pcvrc.com/calculator/heart.php.

Every day, people walk by our house with the intention of staying fit. Unfortunately their walk is not brisk enough and they are not truly exercising (according to the Harvard Medical School and John Hopkins Medical School). Perhaps it is enough that they are enjoying the scenery, but I hope they don't count on their having received a solid workout. I am tempted to stand outside handing out Heartbeatz music and telling this same tale to them.

I should just mind my own business.

Anyway… I know you are in perfect shape for the time being. I was too when I was in college playing conference tennis. But the office with its eating out rewards system started to weigh me down (kind of like a trough). And sooner or later your metabolism just like mine won't be as firey as it is now.

That's when you'll need this Guinea pig reflection. And you'll dig up this email. And get on a treadmill leading to Guinea.

> *Oink,*
> *Your papi*

✉ #35 THINGS I WISH I HAD TAUGHT MY SON… AND STILL CAN
Your words are being tracked…

When we go to fill in that little box in Google, the keywords you enter are registered and tabulated. The same goes for Yahoo and other search engines. Even when you misspell the words, those are being tracked. Today's hottest word searches can be found at Google Hot Trends. For some reason "Selena Death" is the sixth top search today, "Selena's Funeral" is the 11th top search today and "Selena Perez" is the 16th top search today. There is perhaps an airing of the *Selena* movie or a documentary that is playing right now.

I have been writing ads for about 20 years. Before, I wrote ads using my own words, thinking I had some ability to predict how people would react. I was very successful, but my ability to get it right now has risen exponentially. Why? Because I use wordtracker.com. It does something quite amazing. It actually tells me approximately how many people typed in a specific word or group of words into that the little Google box. If people seem to be using that word combination, I consider using it. If people don't use that word combination, I look for something else that may be more effective.

Because I do what I do, many people tell me about the inventions or ideas that they have come up with. They want me to give them feedback as to whether I think it is a viable and potentially profitable idea. My opinion is just that, my opinion. But when I get back to my computer, I can check to see if 12 people are looking for a solution to that specific problem or 12,000. And I can also see if there are already too many competitors offering solutions for that perceived consumer problem. In the next few weeks, I will be selling a PDF download book entitled *The Funeral Planning Checklist*. There are a considerable amount of people typing in those specific words. So I bought funeralplanningchecklist.org and will be creating a website to sell this very comprehensive and money-saving (hundreds to thousands of dollars) book. I didn't write the book. It was written by Marnie McDonald, a life insurance agent who went through the very tedious research process of putting together a book that all indicators suggest will sell quite easily. It will teach people to put their estate in order so that the government doesn't stay with the a large chunk of the family inheritance and so that lawyers don't either. Marnie and I have partnered up to take that book to market. And I will use wordtracker to optimize my site until it gets to the first page rank results on Google.

I am working on a how-to-tie-knots video project with Matt. That will be going to market in the next few weeks too. That product will be on the iPhone as well as on the Internet. I found that a keyword combination that had very few competitors was "tie knots easy". So I bought tieknotseasy.com. I've seen my site in the fourth place slot twice already… Out of 4,000,000 possible sites. It is fighting to stay there. Had I tried to use just "knots" in my meta tag strategy, I would be dwindling somewhere in the 3,000,000th spot.

I'll let you know how both products fare in the marketplace. This will be something that you can do to make money while you pursue the life-fulfilling career of your dreams.

Are you tracking with this?
Your papi

 ### #36 THINGS I WISH I HAD TAUGHT MY SON... AND STILL CAN
What can we learn from marbles?

We called him Cuica... We called him that because he was fast. I guess Cuica is Spanglish for Quick. But he was fast in other ways too.

I used to play marbles as a kid. I would go to Winn's and buy a few fat bags of swirly marbles. We played different types of games. Usually, they were skill-oriented games involving throwing your marble from a distance trying to force other marbles out of an eye-shaped trap. Mostly it was gambling for marbles. If you lost, you lost your marbles.

I remember one specific day that I went over to play marbles with Cuica who was about four to five years older than me. In front of Cuica's house was a solid red dirt clearing perfect for playing marbles. That fateful day, we played "el posito", the little hole. We used a little dugout cup-size hole as the playing venue. Cuica, who had a gallon-sized box, almost three quarters of the way filled with other people's marbles decided he would teach me how to play. I would lose my marbles that day.

The lesson for today: Pay attention to the rules. If your opponent is making the rules, you will probably lose. Know what you're getting into and know when you have been dealt a disadvantaged position. The flip-side of the coin is to make the rules when playing marbles or when playing in business or in any competitive condition. A good example of how Apple does it is with their iPod. The iPod has never been referred to as an mp3 player. It is an iPod. There was the first rule. They also made the rules when they introduced a large format music player that held a whopping 10,000 songs (this was many years ago). All the mp3 players held about 500 songs at the time. They further set the rules when they introduced iTunes, a legal downloading music store that only played on iPods. They further solidified the rules when they added video and multiple colors, and a phone/music player called the iPhone. And meanwhile, all the other mp3 players lost their marbles.

That fateful day, Cuica said, "Gimme two marbles." I did. He took the two marbles in his hand and said, "I'm going to throw these marbles into the hole. Some will stay in. Some will jump out. If what remains inside and outside the hole is an even number of marbles, I win.

If it is odd, you win." He threw the marbles. He won. "Gimme two more marbles." I did. He won again. Then when it looked like I had won because the marbles were distributed one and three or three and one, I didn't. That's when he said something like this, "because I won the last two games, I win this one. If it is odd the next time then you win." I guess you've probably seen this in basketball when playing "make it take it". Regardless, the next marble toss into the hole was probably even and he won. I believe every time I won, there was a changing of the rules until I lost all my marbles.

I now tell this story when I am in front of hundreds of people in marketing seminars. Cuica taught me a valuable lesson. When you take control of the rules, it is much easier to win. When you are able to define the "what is right" and "what is wrong" of something, you can make your product, service or idea the only right choice. Cuica taught me this hard-knock lesson and Paul Goya taught me how to apply the lesson to all the fields of business in which I operate.

I know I recently gave you some writing advice and it didn't go over well with your prof. Unfortunately, your prof controls the rules of the class, and he or she doesn't value the type of writing I believe is more effective. I know I break a whole mess of rules of grammar in these emails. But I can… Because I make the rules here.

> *Don't lose your marbles,*
> *Your papi*

PS: I recently ran into Cuica a few months ago. I told him he was the opening to some of my speeches. I told him that I am paying him back for taking my marbles. He laughed. He didn't remember.

 #37 THINGS I WISH I HAD TAUGHT MY SON… AND STILL CAN
That's a stretch…

I was a cramper. Throughout high school, I got cramps that ran up the back of my legs up through to my back. They were horrible streaks of systematic pain. They haunted me. Sometimes I woke up in the night screaming, only to make them worse.

In Hebbronville and in Laredo, I was accustomed to playing in 100° + heat. Accustomed is probably not the most appropriate word because one wrong move after a tennis match and I was recoiling, wincing, cringing… Looking pretty pathetic.

Then I joined the tennis team while at Laredo Junior College. That's where I met Sara Carasco, our wonderful coach. Perhaps she wasn't the best at tennis strategy but she had a different plan that would help us to win quite frequently.

At first I didn't understand all the stretching exercises. It seemed like we spent way too much time stretching our backs, our shoulders, our calves, our thighs. We stretched every day for 20 to 30 minutes before we even hit the courts. And guess what? Coupled with better nutrition, the cramps faded away into a forgotten chapter of my life. I remember a Nationals Conference tournament that was held in Laredo. We played and won that day like it was a walk in the park. Other players from the north were on the floor screaming in pain from the cramps that crept up on them. I would like to say that we won, but there was one team consisting of giant South African (most were 6'3" tall) players who pounded us. One intimidating thing that they did was jump rope between matches. They weren't fazed by the 114° Laredo heat. Oh well.

The lesson for today is simple. Stretch, stretch and stretch some more. Because you are tall, you may start to hunch over a little like I am beginning to do. Stretching will keep the oxygen flowing through the blood in your muscles. Stretching will protect you when you get older and feel like you want to do some weekend warrior ballin'. Stretching will also help you sleep better. One particular undesirable trait that you may have inherited from me is the turning in of the "rotator cuff". It's a daily dull chronic pain. Now is the only time that you can change the course of that otherwise inevitable malady. Read up on the stretches and posture that can reverse its effects and improve the health of your shoulder and back muscles.

These are just a few tips… Your quest is to find the others.

Gotta stretch now,
Your papi

 ### #38 THINGS I WISH I HAD TAUGHT MY SON… AND STILL CAN
Back-up your digital life…

On the 6th of May at about 6:40 PM, the video surveillance camera at the Avis Rent a Car center adjacent to the Triton Tennis Complex captured the fuzzy images of three to four men wearing white pants and white shirts breaking into my van, taking my computer bag… And about five years of work, writings, etc. Besides my 200 gig portable computer, I usually toted around five additional hard drives, each 100 to 125 gigs in size. I never saw my stuff again.

I had installed a tracking device in the computer but it seemed that it hadn't worked properly in a few months. The provider of the tracking software returned my purchase price of $99 and their apologies. I eventually had to take the reality pill and come to grips with the fact that those missing chapters of my digital life weren't coming back. I had backed-up some of my work, but about 60% is probably in data heaven.

The incidence of theft is going up proportionately with the financial distress people are experiencing in their hometowns, in the country. You experienced identity theft even before your first day of college. Unfortunately, you will experience many more incidences of theft before you get to be my age.

Perhaps you don't think the stuff on your computer or phone is that valuable. I assure you that when you're an old man; you will have a different perspective on this. You will cherish anything you've written, any art you've created, any songs you have composed.

Somewhere in some dusty hard drive, I have kept the little stories you made up when you were a five or six-year-old. You would stand next to me, and I would type whatever nonsensical story you dreamt up and dictated. It's all backed-up.

The lesson for today is "back-up" your stuff. Every time you come home for a visit, make a redundant copy of your computer so that if it is stolen, you don't lose a piece of you, you just lose plastic, silicon, aluminum and a few other composite materials that are used to make a computer.

> *Backing-up now and moving forward,*
> *Your papi*

PS: Don't think for a second that your dorm is a safe storage place. Keep your computer hidden along with any other hock-able items.

 #39 THINGS I WISH I HAD TAUGHT MY SON... AND STILL CAN
One of life's hard knocks.

When I was somewhere in the neighborhood of seven years old, I recall sitting in the passenger seat of my oldest brother's Ford Fairlane. I don't know where we were going, but it involved going past Joel Muñoz' Texaco on the corner of Galbraith and Mesquite in Hebbronville, Texas. Why do I remember that corner so vividly? I fell out of the car when the Fairlane took the turn.

Earlier that day, I had been watching my older brothers flying kites. There were lots of kids at my house looking up into the western sky at their tiny kites. The kites back then were diamond-shaped paper kites with homemade tails made of random scraps of cloth. One of the common kite-flying practices of the day was to not only use one spool of kite string but to combine two or three spools, extending the kite out into the bluest parts of the sky. I thought about this recently when I saw the movie, *The Kite Runner*.

Like I said I don't know where my mom wanted my brother and I to go, but I remember I grudgingly got in the Fairlane against my wishes. The kite-flying event was where I wanted to be. Maybe somebody would let me hold their makeshift (made out of a broom handle) spool. I'm sure I protested about going with my brother. I'm sure I lost. And we were off.

Why I fell out will forever remain a mystery. My memory has played tricks on me, filled in the blanks, even embellished the truth. That's what brains do… They compress, generalize, distort, add and delete details that actually happened or never happened.

But the fact remains that I fell out of a moving car. Or I threw myself out. Or gravity pulled me out.

I don't know if the door was cracked open or defective. I don't know if I had a death wish or had seen one too many stunt movies, causing me to open the door. I just don't remember.

What I do remember is that my brother didn't notice that I was missing for half a block. When I stopped rolling and knocking around on the pavement, I looked at the car speeding away. Then it braked suddenly and my startled brother jumped out, running towards me. Joel Muñoz sprinted out of his gasoline station to help me up. I was alright. I had a long scrape along my leg, hip and side, but it was a surface wound. I think I also skinned my elbow.

We returned home. The kite-flyers came to see what all the commotion was about, but they lost interest right away and got back to their kites.

I didn't get to watch them the rest of the day. They kept me inside, interrogating me.

You may be wondering what the heck the lesson is for today. It's one I've got to work on just as much as you. It's one that I have to keep top-of-mind when I get into my van. I need to strap on the seat belt. I need to make it a no-brainer habit. You do to, especially when somebody else is driving.

Now fasten your seat belt for your upcoming Biology test,

    Your papi

#40 THINGS I WISH I HAD TAUGHT MY SON... AND STILL CAN
Sometimes things can spread...

A few days ago, I received an email that I had received several years prior. The email told the story of an Scottish farmer named Fleming who saved the son of a nobleman. The boy had been trapped in a bog and the farmer freed him from a slow and terrible death. The nobleman tries to repay the farmer, but the farmer doesn't accept. Then, the nobleman notices the son of the farmer as he comes out of the family hovel, which is another word for shack, and suggests a different deal.

The nobleman offers to provide the fine level of education to the farmer's boy that his own son will receive. The nobleman states, "If the lad is anything like his father, he'll no doubt grow to be a man we both will be proud of." The farmer accepts the offer.

In the email account, Farmer Fleming's son attends the very best schools. He graduates from St. Mary's Hospital Medical School in London. He goes on to become known throughout the world as Sir Alexander Fleming, the discoverer of penicillin.

The email further mentions that the boy who was pulled from the bog and contracts pneumonia later in life. What saves the boy's life is penicillin. Who was this boy? According to the chain email, the boy was the son of Lord Randolph Churchill, the famous Sir Winston Churchill.

It's a beautiful story of "what goes around comes around". Unfortunately, it never happened.

But this story does have a happy ending, at least in my book. Penicillin saved somebody infinitely more important than Winston Churchill. You see, I was born on Alexander Fleming's birthday. But I wouldn't have been born if Alexander hadn't invented penicillin because this antibiotic saved my father's life in 1945 during World War II. And if I hadn't been born, neither would have you. And so although this fable will continue to arrive in in-boxes around the world, know that a boy from Lochfield farm near Darvel in East Ayrshire, Scotland accidentally discovered penicillin and changed the world with his Vújà De. It certainly changed our lives.

Here's to Alex,
Your papi

 #41 THINGS I WISH I HAD TAUGHT MY SON... AND STILL CAN
Today is not an ordinary day...

I met a young man last year that said, "This is the best day of my life." J.P. went on to tell me that "today" is the only day he has. What he meant by this is that "today" is the only day that he, you and I can live fully. Yesterday is gone, tomorrow may never come. Today is today and it will be as good as you and I can make it.

Often, people live in the past. They dwell on some event that came and went. They spend hours reflecting on that pivotal event. Yet, they can't do anything about that past event. Often, while distracted by the past, they miss out on making "today" the best that it can be. One of the guys at our breakfast hangout lets the results of the weekend's Dallas Cowboy game set the tone for the week. I'm sure he misses a few "todays" when they Cowboys miss one pass or one tackle too many.

Some people worry about what happened yesterday. Some people eagerly wait on the doorsteps of tomorrow. That's when they've decided that they'll really live. For some of these people though, tomorrow never arrives. Yet today is actually yesterday's tomorrow.

I've lost contact with J.P. I know he once crossed the country in his car, living in it, exploring the nooks and crannies of the United States. If I were to take a wild guess, J.P. is traveling the world right about now. And I suspect that today was the best day of his life.

As for me… Today was the best day of my life too. I spoke with each of my children. I spoke with my wife, my dad too. I even caught the end of one of his Spanish novelas. I spoke with my friends. I wrote. I completed a *My Story* movie about a Guatemalan couple. I built a website. I learned a new trick on Google Adwords. I enjoyed a new audio book with three of my kids, *The 39 Clues* (we're listening to it on the way to school in the mornings). I talked to Hope, our beagle. The list goes on… And it's only 11 PM.

The lesson for today is to not waste your "todays".

> *Live like today is the best day of your life,*
> *Your papi*

 #42 THINGS I WISH I HAD TAUGHT MY SON… AND STILL CAN
When life takes a turn, lean with it…

Sometimes things don't go the way you plan. Sometimes, setbacks you never expected reroute your schedule, even your life. Don't fret this stuff. Perhaps you may not have control over when and why these unforeseeable situations will occur, but you will have total control over how you respond to them.

This morning, as I loaded my computer into my backpack, I noticed a rattling inside my computer. I knew immediately that your little sister had struck again. I pulled a quarter and two pennies from the CD/DVD drive of my computer. This little sister of yours has also taken apart my glasses three times. They were irreparable. I didn't plan for these blinding setbacks, and I didn't hang that little monster upside down from her toes. Come to think of it, she isn't unique. I remember when I put you and your next youngest sister on the interrogation hot seat. I had in my hand our busted video camera. You were about five and your sister about three. Both of you denied involvement. It's almost as if you had a pact to defend each other and keep quiet. Very convenient.

Mom is running frantically because your second youngest brother just came home sick today with a potential stomach flu (that can take out the whole family). She had no room for that hiccup in her schedule. But hey… Nothing has gone right this week anyway, according to her.

Olivia (your sister's friend, our friend) started cancer treatment yesterday. At 16, her plans have definitely not gone as she planned them. She has already spent several horrible months in horrendous chemotherapy trying to beat the Leukemia in her body. After a few months of being absent, it's back. This time her younger sister Julia is going to sacrifice some of her bone marrow to help get her sister's life back on track.

Olivia came up to me two days ago (during her sister's volleyball game) to give me her schedule for the next few weeks and months (her chemo and bone marrow transplant). She came to thank us for the prayers we have dedicated to her, her family and her healing. Judging from her spirits, she understands that she doesn't have control over her medical condition, but she does have total control over how she can respond to it. She chooses to be audaciously hopeful. She chooses to be strong in her resolve. She chooses to make others happy. Go Olivia! Teach us all.

Pray for Olivia,
Your papi

 #43 THINGS I WISH I HAD TAUGHT MY SON… AND STILL CAN
Old dogs can learn new trick words…

I had a horrible vocabulary when I graduated from high school. No… I didn't use foul language. I just had a very shallow choice of words at my disposal for my writing projects. When people didn't use common words, I often didn't know what they were talking about. In college especially, professors tended to use 50¢ and 75¢ words that went over my head. I think I missed a lot because I hadn't crossed paths with many exotic words in my formative years.

Then the Internet happened to me.

It is so easy now to catapult your vocabulary. Whenever you hear an unfamiliar word, you can Google it. Immediately, you are presented with options. You may be presented with a Wikipedia or Wiktionary page. From not knowing what a word means, you can fast-forward to expert status in the matter of a minute. Before the Internet, the same task would require hunting down a dictionary, spotting the word in that 500 page (small print) book and then writing it out or typing it out depending upon what your project called for. Now you can Google the word, click a hyperlink, read the definition, copy it, paste it, and paraphrase it in one breath. It's a snap. Usually you can do all this in the same time it would take you to just find your misplaced dictionary were you still doing it the old-school way.

Something else happened along the way. I grew very fond of finding the right words for the right projects. And I have also become a neologist (look it up, Google it), and a budding etymologist. Etymology is the study of the origin and historical development of a word(s). Before discovering etymology, I never realized that all words were "coined" or made-up at some point in history by somebody like you or me. There are also people that usually document when these words first appeared, how they were used and from what archaic language they originated. During this word adventure, I also came to find out that our English language is composed 50% of Latin and 30% of Greek.

The lesson for today is how to practically absorb new words into your personal lexicon. This is what I did about five to six years ago.

I went to yourdictionary.com and at the bottom of the screen, signed up for the free word of the day. It arrives religiously every day. I read it, let the meaning sink in. And I always make sure I read the etymology section of the email. That, coupled with the substantial amount of reading that I do, has filled my well of words. Hey, you never know when you're going to be on a game show.

> *Word up,*
> *Your papi,*

PS: The word today was mugwump.

PSS: Your two sisters had phenomenal games in front a very packed gym. They won. They were confident. It was intense.

✉ #44 THINGS I WISH I HAD TAUGHT MY SON... AND STILL CAN
This one is hot!

By the time I was a freshman in high school, I had already been initiated into the world of serranos, jalapeños and pequin peppers. Hector Almaraz and I would ride around our small town with a rather large heaping of jalapeños balanced on top of our Dairy Queen melted cheese nachos. Sometimes we got tangled up with some very angry peppers. We howled and downed lots of liquids... Then we continued. My cousin Oscar and I would always dare each other as 12 or 13-year-olds to eat from the wild chile pequin bush that grew behind my dad's gas station. That was life threatening hot stuff. But, it was like a rite of passage for two young Mexican-American boys. It was supposed to grow hair on my chest. I'm still waiting.

In 1912, Wilbur Scoville devised the Scoville Organoleptic Test. He created this test for rating the pungency of chili peppers. In other words, he did it to measure the hotness of different types of peppers. Oddly enough, chiles (peppers) are fruits. They are from the genus Capsicum and contain something called capsaicin (the hot stuff). This chemical compound stimulates chemoreceptor nerve endings in the skin and mucous membranes.

The Scoville rating method utilizes an extract of the pepper diluted in a sugary syrup. Five taste testers sample the sugary solution until they can't detect any "hotness". The degree of dilution that renders the pepper un-hot becomes the measure on the Scoville scale.

Sweet peppers have a rating of 0. They contain no capsaicin. Pimento has a little bit of capsaicin, it rates in at 100 to 500 scoville units. The poblano pepper used in chile rellenos has a rating from 500 to 2,500. I'm a little disappointed that jalapeños only rate in the 2,500 to 8,000 range (kind of demoralizing since I thought I was hot stuff). The serrano and chipotle weighs in between 10,000 and 23,000. Cayenne, aji, chipotle and the tabasco (not the bottled version) climb to the 30 to 50,000 level. The deadly pequin that my cousin Oscar and I toyed with is a tiny concentration of 50,000 to 100,000 scoville units. The habanero family soars into the 100,000 to 580,000 range. I once almost hyperventilated when I ate a sauce made of habaneros at Mi Cocina in Dallas. I was tricked by some cruel friends. It's hard to believe that anything could be hotter than the habanero. The naga jolokai and dorset naga are probably nuclear hot climbing into the millionth scoville mark. Pepper spray, the kind that is sprayed into people's eyes for protection, is 2,000,000 to 5,500,000 scoville units hot. Oooooooouuuuuuuch!

Finally, pure capsaicin is 15 million to 16 million units hot, the end of the world.

I don't know if you've explored the more exquisite piquancy moments in life. It would seem that I am a bit heartless if I recommend you go out and explore your Scoville threshold.

Yet, that is precisely what this lesson is about. Taste the pungency. WARNING: I have a friend named Emma from college who ate 110 jalapeños in one sitting during Borderfest in Laredo. I don't recommend that kind of exploration. No, I just encourage you to research why your ancestors willingly self-inflicted so much pain during their meals. Was it for pain or pleasure? Was it rational? Was it just for tradition? Find out.

And keep the tradition going!

>*Ouch, delicious,*
>*Your papi*

PS:　It'll grow hair on your chest!

 #45 THINGS I WISH I HAD TAUGHT MY SON... AND STILL CAN
Pay attention to your spilling...

I hate to **mispell** words. When somebody sends me **mispelled** words, I get distracted by there **carelessless**. Teachers hate incorrect spellings too. True, some will **overlok** it but most will take it personally, deeming you somebody who doesn't care enough to run **spelcheck**.

The earliest evidence of the phrase "Spelling Bee" goes back to 1825. However, spelling bees were informally taking place before that. If we were living in a time before Noah Webster cornered the market with his spelling books, different people would probably still be spelling words differently. The Webster spelling books became a force for the standardization of spelling. Webster's *The Blue-backed Speller* was used as the reference for judging whether a spelling bee contestant was right or wrong. And for five generations, these books were used as an essential part of the curriculum of all elementary school children.

Nowadays, these newfangled computers are tracking along with you as you type, letting you no that it **thhinks** you have misspelled a word. Most email programs will do the same. Microsoft Word does it, Pages does it. Some webmail sites do it too. If you misspell a word today, it is because you are lazy or dyslexic. The first can be avoided through the use of technology and reference dictionaries and I'm sure that there are some technologies that can help people with dyslexia.

Therefore, if you notice as you type that your screen looks like a it is hemorrhaging, chances are that you **hav misspellled** a few words and should go back to correct them. As it stands now, this email has eight underlined words. There will probably be more before I finish. But I've done this deliberately to make a point. And I know that I have used several words with correct spellings in this email while they remain the wrong word usage for the sentence.

The lesson for today... Run spell-check. It will send a clear message to your reader that you care enough to remove the distractions from your writing.

Putting a spell on you,
Your papi

PS: Spelling is a lifelong skill that you become more adept at with practice. It is like a mussel that eventually gets stronger. Or is it a like muscle that eventually gets stronger?

 #46 THINGS I WISH I HAD TAUGHT MY SON... AND STILL CAN
Catch people doing things right...

One of these days, probably sooner than you think, you will be in a leadership position. People will value positive feedback from you the way you value positive feedback from those you respect. The right positive feedback at the right time can exponentially boost a person's confidence. Your words might have the power to get a person over a hump of life, helping them start an exhilarating ride through life with polished self confidence.

I've already written about the power of words. Today's lesson is about the power of the right moment to use those words.

Until about four years ago, peaceful nights were interrupted and replaced with loud nerve-racking feelings of defenselessness. On these startling nights, overhead flying helicopters woke us up shining an occasional spotlight into our bedroom window. Distant sirens getting closer added to the made-for-TV-like drama. Our perception was that it always seemed that we were in the very middle of the police search. Was the perpetrator on foot? In the backyard? In a car in our driveway? Inside our neighbor's house? We knew nothing, just that random lights lit up our house. Without any type of closure as to what the chase was about or whether the police had apprehended the suspect, getting back to sleep was a chore. Getting through work sleep deprived the next day was not fun either. Often, we would never hear anything about the incident on the news nor in the newspaper. For some reason, these helicopter chases have subsided. Thank God. Perhaps satellites have replaced the helicopter. After all, you can see the top of our house on the Internet via Google Earth. I don't know what has replaced the choppers. I'm just glad that they're gone.

There is something to learn from these overhead chop-chop-chop-chop-choppers. When you are working with others you should pretend to be a search helicopter. No, I don't suggest you be like Bill Lumbergh from *Office Space*, looking to catch people doing things wrong. I propose you be like a helicopter scanning and searching for people doing things right. Rest assured that people will be doing things right often. However, if they are never noticed, it won't matter as much. Our society and prevailing management style in the work place seems to concentrate more on punishing people for doing things wrong rather than recognizing people who excel.

> *Chop-chop,*
> *Your papi*

 #47 THINGS I WISH I HAD TAUGHT MY SON... AND STILL CAN
If you want to learn something... Teach it.

Having trouble in school? Find somebody who is struggling with a subject that you are having trouble with and try to help him or her. The added pressure of having to learn a subject matter well enough to teach it will make you learn it more integrally. I don't know where or when I first heard this concept, but I know I thought it was quite dumb. How can I teach something that I don't know? Well, you learn it! Duh!

I have adopted this mantra for life, now. Sometimes I get myself waist-high, even neck-high into unchartered muddy waters. But if I trudge long enough and smart enough through it while I drag someone along, I learn something. Actually, I learn it well. I must feel, in the back of my mind, that if I don't "get it", I will have a witness that saw me fail. Perhaps that's good motivation. I don't want to look dumb.

Teaching something also makes you learn because you have to explain it clearly... Clearly enough that it even makes sense to you. If you can accomplish this, then you're on your way to chiseling the knowledge into your brain, not just memorizing it so that it disappears after the quiz or test.

The flip-side of teaching to learn is that you have to adopt better student skills. The best teachers are those who are great students themselves. Those who have put their learning on pause or stop can be dangerous to the students entrusted to them. Most of the time, fear is the governing emotion that stunts new learning, "I better not learn this new technology because I'm afraid I might not "get it". Always watch out for that liar called fear.

I'm learning a great deal writing these emails. I feel alive, like I'm moving with life, not getting left behind. I'm quite surprised with the reservoir of ideas that I didn't know were waiting to be channeled into streams of learning. I'm going to continue learning so that I can continue teaching so that I can continue learning.

> *Class is out early today,*
> *Your papi*

#48 THINGS I WISH I HAD TAUGHT MY SON… AND STILL CAN
Appreciate your mami…

I can juggle three tennis balls. A few of my friends can juggle four balls. Other more accomplished jugglers can work with five to seven balls. Then they get more complicated with bowling pins, rings, lit torches, hatchets, knives and swords… Or a combination of different items like torches and balls and knives all at the same time. Sometimes they juggle under their legs, over their backs, on a unicycle, etc.

Well, your mom has them beat. She can juggle eight kids, a goldfish, two cats, a guitar, a video camera, a booster club, a still camera, a part-time job, 400 mismatched socks, a pack of Hot Pockets, four Happy Meals, three or four friends, several daily fires, a quirky husband, a visiting skunk, three sisters, a few unread newspapers, a bouncy checking account, five backpacks and a box of wipies with a Purell chaser. Wow… What a woman.

Your mom is at a retreat this weekend and won't be home 'til Sunday. That seems like 10 years from now. How she manages to know where lost shoes are in the morning… How she can know when your brother has a spelling test, or your sister has an out-of-town game is beyond me. This morning was a challenge. Your smallest brother, right before we left for school dumbfounded me when he asked, "Where's my lunch?"

It threw me into a tailspin. "What do you eat?" I asked. He rattled out a lot of stuff that we didn't have in the refrigerator or pantry. I managed to stick a few odd things in his lunchbox that he found acceptable. Thank God your other brothers and sisters eat at the cafeteria.

So we go off to school and as I walk him to his front door and get my kiss, just like every other day, I notice something is very wrong.. That's when I notice his shirt is stained… And not a little insignificant maybe-they-won't-see-it stain. No, this was a baked-in mixed media piece of art primarily using an expressive red sauce. It created a vertical stripe down his right chest. At the same time, the teacher opens the door and notices the terror on my face. "Uhmm, uhmm, uhmm, uhmm," I say as she tries to read my incoherent mind. She finally notices why I'm distressed. I tell her that I asked him to find a shirt and that he found one, just not a clean one. She promises to look the other way. And I drive away like the absent-minded professor in *Flubber*.

Your mom is amazing. I just did the math and I estimate that with you alone, she changed 4,020 diapers. Have you ever thanked her for that? Multiply that by eight and she has probably hovered in the 32,000 diapers changed range. Of course I changed your diapers too but not in these astronomical numbers. I didn't stay up nearly as much as she did whenever you were attacked by the flu or by allergies or by those mysterious stomach cramps that plagued you in middle school.

The lesson for today is to make today, tomorrow, the day-after-tomorrow and every day thereafter Mother's Day. Don't wait for the commercialized Mother's Day Sunday to write her a five minute poem and give her an on-cue hug and kiss. And when she calls to give you motherly advice, be kind, don't fidget, honor her words and remember she put you first always... The way mother's tend to do.

Happy Mother's Day in October,
Your papi

PS: Don't call today... She'll be back on Sunday. But you can come home and help with the kids.

 #49 THINGS I WISH I HAD TAUGHT MY SON... AND STILL CAN
God and the left-brainers...

I've copied and pasted this next excerpt from a the website about.com:

QUESTION: Haven't scientists, philosophers, and theologians proven that God exists?

ANSWER: No, God's existence has not been proven, so atheism is reasonable.

The article later goes on to say this... "Even the best arguments defending the existence of God are full of problems, holes, and logical errors. Most of the time they seem to be more about helping believers rationalize and justify beliefs they already hold rather than to provide a sound foundation for adopting a belief."

I went to about.com, but I could have gone to many different sites to find something similar to the aforementioned.

Remember Cuica from #36, the guy that made me lose my marbles? He was the one that made the rules and changed the rules after every game. Atheists think we've lost our marbles too if we believe in God, a god, or a Divine Creator. That's because they're playing the same marble game with us that Cuica played on me when I was a kid. They make the rules of the game. They change the rules of the game. They win. How does the game work? Logically. The game-board is the scientific method. Scientists who seek to disprove God use the rational, experimental "proof" approach to push the reader, the listener, the non PhD scientist into a corner, making him or her believe "I'm stupid" and science is the Savior of the world. Paul Goya taught me that by accepting their frame, their rules, it is impossible to be right. In their game, only scientists are right.

There is a recent popular book called *The God Delusion* written by Richard Dawkins. I haven't read it yet (I'm waiting for it to be a 1¢), but I will. I'll read it, and I won't doubt the existence of God. Why? Because I'm not half-brained. Logical analytical thinking is a left brain dominant type of thinking. I use all my brain to fathom God. I heard Richard Dawkins frame his argument on the radio the other day. While he uses sound analytical, deductive reasoning, that's all he uses. I bet with those rules, he could also prove that a mother's love does not exist either… Or any kind of love for that matter.

Jodi Foster had a hard time with God in *Contact*. She was a left brain scientist in the movie who could not consider God outside of a test tube context. Then she has an experience with the memory of her dead father. Was it real? Empirical? At the end, the viewer is left empty-handed. Is what she experienced God or some mental delusion. Did she lose her marbles?

The lesson for today is to not get caught in a word trap discussion about God. Change the rules. Allow intuition, symbolic thought and creative thought to be fair game in the discussion. After all he is our Creator. If some atheist can prove to you that God doesn't exist, agree with him or her. I too will agree that in a half-brained world, God definitely does not exist.

The following is Albert Einstein's response to a famous atheist. This is what I call a full-brained orientation towards God: "Try and penetrate with our limited means the secrets of nature and you will find that, behind all the discernible concatenations, there remains something subtle, intangible and inexplicable. Veneration for this force beyond anything that we can comprehend is my religion. To that extent I am, in point of fact, religious." — Albert Einstein, Response to atheist, Alfred Kerr (1927).

> *Thank God,*
> *Your papi*

PS: When I was in school, Pluto was a planet. Oops! Now there are only eight. I want my planet back.

 #50 THINGS I WISH I HAD TAUGHT MY SON… AND STILL CAN
Never let anybody tell you what you believe.

College is fertile ground for recruiters seeking new members for their ideology. One of the leading strategies for a person to put his ideology in a better light is to put yours in a negative light. Often people that do this will pluck a few random ideas related to your belief system (your religion) and quote them out of context leaving you doubting. Unless you're familiar with this type of attack you may get caught off-guard and feel duped by your parents, by the institutions who formed your character, by your church. Disorientation is the desired response these people seek. Then they can plant the seeds of their ideology, water it, and watch it grow. It happens every day.

In the Spanish language, there is a distinct word for a live fish. It is a *pes*. When it is caught and is dead, it is called a *pescado*. We have a fish (a pes). It's other name is Fishy (not a very creative name but oh well). Fishy is a goldfish. We got the fish when it was small, but it has grown quite large. If we were to take Fishy out of its tank and place it on the kitchen counter, Fishy would have a hard time. It would flap around, wiggle, open its mouth in an effort to cycle water through its gills. Within a few minutes Fishy (pes) would be dead (pescado). This is not a Spanish lesson, it is a lesson about context. To Fishy, the water tank is its context. Similarly, taking a passage out of its context in the Bible or taking a piece (or historical event) of the belief system that we have passed on to you out of its context is like taking Fishy out of water. An idea out of context will be weak and die. I have had members of other religions try to tell me what I believe. They point out obscure specifics about my religion that simply aren't true (but that would require some research to refute). They have a script. It sounds sound. And meanwhile, I'm reduced to silly putty.

Mess with their script and they can lose their place.

Once when I was a freshman in college, I was walking down a street in Laredo. A man stopped me and asked if I knew what the following verses said: John 16:15-19 (these are not the actual verses... Hey it was a long time ago). I could have felt really inferior for not knowing that scripture but instead a flash arrived. I asked him if he knew what it said in Ecclesiastes 13:22-31 (not the actual verses). He said he didn't know. I then told him I didn't know either, but I went on to tell him that he shouldn't make people feel ignorant because they don't know a specific number passage from the *Bible*. After all, there are thousands of passages.

When somebody tries to undermine your faith, your belief system, pay attention to their style, their approach, their motive. If it smells fishy (pescado) it probably is. If they pretend to be experts (because they saw *Religious* or the *Da Vinci Code*) even though they've never shared the same faith or deep-dived into the doctrine, it's probably fishy too. However if they do succeed at making you feel like your faith foundation is shaky, give me a call. I've heard almost all of the sneaky baits that have been used over the centuries to hook young men and women into other ideologies. I love to learn new ones. More often than not, I'll be able to easily point out how your well-meaning friends have used a stinky fish strategy to frame the discussion and fool you.

> *Do they still call freshmen fish?*
> *Your papi*

✉ **#51 THINGS I WISH I HAD TAUGHT MY SON… AND STILL CAN**
It's a college tradition.

In 1983, I had a four-door '74 Chevy Impala (with a nice dent) that was also the transport vehicle for all the Latin American tennis players living on campus. It was a six passenger car with about nine passengers packed snuggly inside on a late night mission to the H-E-B grocery store in downtown Laredo. All had limited income and large appetites. All spent most of their time pondering what flavor of Ramen noodles they would pick this time. In 1983, a single pack of Ramen noodles cost 13¢. Today, I just checked the website (meijer.com) that sells Ramen noodles in bulk. I couldn't believe that it still costs about 19¢. Twenty five years later and the price has only gone up a mere 6¢. Wow. Meanwhile, the price of gas has gone up from $1.20 in 1983 to almost $4. Ramen gives the McDonald's value meal a run for its money.

If you haven't fully initiated yourself into the sacred tradition of eating Ramen noodles when you've only got 60¢ to your name, know that the annals of college history wait anxiously for you to join its pages.

One day… One very enlightening day in 1988 or 89 I walked into the first giant hall of the Museo de Antropologia in Mexico City. My attention was drawn to a large poster with a headline that read La Mancha Mongolia… The Mongolian (birth) Mark. A flat map of the world had Asia shaded in and furthermore, Texas was shaded in along with Mexico, Central America and half of South America. My mom had always told me that I was born with La Mancha Mongolia, but I had no idea what she meant nor did she ever elaborate beyond those three words. This mancha or birthmark was prominently featured on my Lumbosachral region. In other words, it was on my buttocks. I would later pass that trait on to at least three of my children (I'll protect their identity), maybe four… I don't remember. This bluish gray or brownish patch is present at birth but fades away at about age two. It is common in 96% of black infants, 90% of Native-American infants, 81%-90% of Asian infants, 46-70% Latino infants and only 10% of White infants.

That fateful day in Mexico, all of a sudden everything made sense. I think that's why I liked Ramen noodles so much in college. This Mancha Mongolia connected me to my Asian heritage.

Ramen noodles are mostly considered to be of Chinese origin. Then Japan and other Asian countries piggybacked on the tasty tradition. Real ramen noodles, however, are quite a different thing altogether from their 19¢ distant cousin, just like real spaghetti is very different from the Kraft version. Actually, I'm not sure if I have ever tasted real ramen. Perhaps that will be the subject of a different email. Today's hand-me-down lesson is to savor the high salt, high starch and MSG laden ramen instant noodle that was invented by the late Momofuku

Ando in 1958. All you need is hot water and you'll be cooking. I also remember getting creative with my ramen concoctions by draining the water and adding ham, a little milk and who knows what else. I can almost taste those memories right now. Hey, I was hungry. It was tasty. And by dusk the next day, the starch was converted into energy on the tennis court.

I'm not suggesting that you eat ramen every day, just that you understand its heritage in college dorms and apartments.

> *Sayonara,*
> *Your papi*

PS: In solidarity with my college brethren, I took a break from this email and opened a bag of Ramen. It wasn't as good as I remember it. Oh well… Sometimes memories are tastier than the real thing.

PSS: Instant Ramen was named the greatest Japanese invention of the 20th century in a Japanese poll.

 #52 THINGS I WISH I HAD TAUGHT MY SON… AND STILL CAN
Curiosity killed the cat… But it had eight more lives left.

Nobody can learn you. Learning is something that happens when you're "on". Your professors profess (sort of). Your teachers teach. But they can't learn you. Their responsibility, and why I am willing to support your college learning adventure and corresponding tuition, is to awaken a deep and insatiable curiosity within you. When I got to college, I didn't know the first thing about psychology. But a powerful teacher made me want to find out everything about it. It helped that he was deeply interested in the subject and that he wanted to transfer his love and curiosity to his students.

Now lets talk about Curious George for a bit. I loved Curious George as a kid. I remember exactly on what shelf the two Curious George books lived at our elementary library in Hebbronville, Texas. There was something about that pesky monkey that I could relate to. I didn't really know the details of the story until recently. I just knew from the pictures that he was good at finding trouble… And that he had a yellow-outfitted, yellow-hatted friend. Now that I've seen the movie, I think Curious George rocks. After all, he saved the museum from being closed down and saved the day. The point of this lesson is that curiosity usually precedes learning even though it can get you in trouble sometimes (like George).

Your job in college is to explore the academic subjects that make you want to learn more. Your job is also to "be there" when your profs are on. They may not be on all the time, but when they are, they can change the way you look at things for the rest of your life.

As for the cat that died from its curiosity, there is a story of Blackie reported in the *Washington Post* on March 4th, 1916. Blackie the cat lived in a New York City apartment building on the fifth floor. He often liked to play in the fireplace, but he never went up the flue to the chimney. Well, curiosity got the best of him and he went up. He perched himself on the screen separating the apartment flue from the main chimney. He wouldn't come down. He couldn't come down (I guess cats are chickens about that sort of thing). The next day the cat climbs higher but falls four floors. Eventually a plumber tears out the wall and pulls out the curious Blackie. Unfortunately, the fall was too traumatic. Blackie dies 10 minutes after being rescued.

I guess I was just curious as to why people use the proverb, "Curiosity killed the cat" that warns against being too inquisitive.

The lesson for today is to be curious, but not in a cat-like way. Never confuse the kind of curiosity that inspires and empowers for the one that destroys and robs you of opportunity or life.

Actually, curiosity comes from the Latin word curious meaning careful.

> *Be careful and curious,*
> *Your papi*

PS: Cats are said to have nine lives because they often seem to escape from harrowing life-threatening situations.

 **#53 THINGS I WISH I HAD TAUGHT MY SON... AND STILL CAN
They like to talk... And talk...**

I'm not being a male chauvinist when I say that wives like to talk. About 15 years ago, your mom and I read a book called *His Needs, Her Needs: Building an Affair Proof Marriage*. We read it together and discussed it. We still use the lessons from that book in classes that we give to couples preparing to wed.

His Needs, Her Needs was about the top needs of married couples, and how to satisfy those needs before somebody else does. The book was written by Willard E. Harley Jr. If I remember correctly, the ideas put forth in the book were taken from surveys conducted with about 10,000 couples. In other words, it wasn't his biased opinion. These men and women seemed to converge on five major needs that the men looked for and five major needs that the women had in common. Interestingly, none of the top five needs were shared by the other gender. And most of the time, the men concentrated on trying to please their wives by solving the wrong needs... And the inverse was true for women assuming that their needs were the same needs their husbands valued.

On another day, I will write about the #1 need of women (at least for these 10,000 couples). Today I'm interested in transferring what I learned from the #2 need... Her need for conversation.

There are few women that have ever disagreed with me on this conclusion of Dr. Harley's. Meanwhile, guys tend to think this conversation thing is a real inconvenience. They don't know what the big deal is if they leave out all the pesky details of their work day or if they don't listen to her play by play account of what the teacher said about little Ricky. Many of my friends and family members have had babies. For some odd reason, I usually find out before your mom. I get the call. Not once have I ever been able to answer all the detailed questions your mom has asked me about the dimensions of the baby, the exact time it was born, the hospital it was born at, the color of its eyes, the amount of hair on its head (and color, and amount), the pain involved, the amount of labor, the drive to the hospital, epidural or not, natural or Caesarean, whether the water busted at home, on the way or at the hospital, and the list goes on. I'll get it right one of these days.

As for you, never underestimate the value most women place on face-to-face, comprehensive, and completely engaged (being there) dialogue. The word comes from the Greek dialogos which means to converse with...

I know you're not a talker. Perhaps that is a muscle you'll need to develop. Trust me on this one... I know that if you earnestly develop this converse-ability, it will greatly improve the chances that your soul mate will travel with you the entire journey... All the way into the sunset.

Express yourself,
Your papi

PS: Olivia got her bone marrow transplant yesterday... She will be entering rough waters in a few days as her immune system will be non-existent. Pray for her. Also, pray for Albert Sanchez' mom who had a stroke on Saturday and then again yesterday.

✉ #54 THINGS I WISH I HAD TAUGHT MY SON... AND STILL CAN
Beware... They're everywhere...

(Make sure you read this whole email or don't read any of it)

Be careful with the Terraminga spider. I heard this from a friend at work who has a cousin that goes to a Texas university. Apparently the Biology department of that university was interbreeding the Two-Striped Telamonia spider and the common Black Widow at this undisclosed campus (it could be yours). Recent accounts have been reported that the university in question is threatening anybody who tries to reveal its identity. What I heard, and I believe it because my friend's son was going to that university and knew some of the Biology students, is that the Biology department was next to the largest dorm on the campus. This happened in 2004, and the spider has been breeding since then. The new Terraminga spider is reaching maturity. According to Ty Arana, editor of the *Arachnophobist Journal*, the deadly spiders will reach maturity in 2008. The university has so much to lose if this gets out. They've tried to stop several blogs who were warning students about this. It's a PR nightmare that they don't want to have. I want you to come home. Forget your books. Please leave your backpack, it may have a nest of this spider's eggs.

OK... OK... What you just read above I just made up. Nothing of what you just read is true. There is a Two Striped Telamonia spider, and there is a Black Widow. There is no Terraminga spider. Ty Arana is not a real person. The *Arachnophobist Journal* doesn't exist. I invented that publication a few minutes ago. Although some of the story above could be likely, none of it is true.

There are so many stories like the one above circulating on the world wide web (this is a different kind of web). They are similar in that there is always some voice of authority like Ty Arana and some personal account of a friend whose father or cousin saw it with his own eyes. Sometimes they are cautionary tales that prey on this country's fears. Very often, they deceive and by the time they are deemed to be a hoax, they have circulated the world. College students tend to forward many of these horrendous tales like the one of the guy who drank something at a bar and later woke up in a tub of ice, a note that says to call an ambulance and his kidneys missing. One of the last email tales that I got was about the Amero, a new secret currency that is being minted by our government because the dollar is about to collapse. I got this email complete with a YouTube.com video this very morning.

If you ever feel like something fits this too-strange and too-fishy-to-be-real criteria, go to snopes.com. This website spends all of its time debunking urban legends. In the span of a minute or two, you'll know if what you just received is a warning you should heed or an email you should trash.

Snopes.com is a really good resource. And I predict that urban legend writers are going to include in their text that "even snopes.com has confirmed that this is not a hoax" in the plot of their deceptive story. If they say that, go to snopes.com anyway and confirm it for yourself. There will be a red False after the word status or a red True. The web page will explain the rest of the story.

Every time I receive an urban legend-sounding email, I research it. If I find it to be false, I respond to the sender and let them know where they can go to validate future "the sky is falling" warnings. It's embarrassing to be called on it. I used to fall for the bait back in the day. I used to hit "forward" and "send" when I was new to emailing (hey, if its in print, it must be true). Don't get tangled in this web of deceit. But clean your backpack just in case.

> *This email will self-destruct in five minutes (Just kidding),*
> *Your papi*

 #55 THINGS I WISH I HAD TAUGHT MY SON... AND STILL CAN
Books dot com are cheaper...

You can save a lot of money if you buy your books online or at a Half-Price bookstore. Often, when it comes to college books, you know well in advance when you'll need a particular book. Don't stall. Go to amazon.com and see if the book is available there. It will usually take a week to arrive. Many times, you'll be able to buy the book for 15¢ plus shipping. Actually that is a little deceiving since most booksellers that sell stuff for 15¢ or 25¢ do that so their book will be at the top of the used book list. Instead, they make their money from the over-inflated shipping price. Still, compared to the prices at a new book store, you still save a load of money.

Amazon.com is a nightmare for publishers and writers but a slice of heaven for readers. You can amass a great library with relatively little money. Another two good sites are alibris.com and bn.com.

During your college years you will need to buy many books. Don't pay full price. Use the sites I suggest or type in the exact name of the book you are needing. You may find it even cheaper.

One last thing before I close this email.

I have an account with questia.com. Questia is like having your own research library complete with books, professional journals, magazine articles and so forth. Actually it has 67,000 full-text books and 1.5 million complete journal, magazine and newspaper articles.

Check it out,
Your papi

#56 THINGS I WISH I HAD TAUGHT MY SON... AND STILL CAN
When you get to the fork in the road...

Although our modern forks have four prongs, that's not the fork I'm writing about. A fork in the road is a metaphor for coming to a point in your day, your semester, your career, your life. It is the point where you take one path or the other and accept the positive or negative consequences that come with it. Some forks in the road will literally be about what you decide to eat for lunch (in which case you may use a regular fork). Others will be about who your soul mate will be. Some will have unnoticeable consequences. Others will move your life forward or set it back.

We usually try to weigh all the information we have when we make a choice. Do we feel informed enough? Is there some missing piece of information that can help us make the decision? We pay attention to our emotions, too. Are we confident enough with ourselves to take on the tougher road? If we don't take the tougher road, does it make us weaker the next time we come to a new fork in the road? If we do take the harder road and succeed, does it make us more prepared to take on even bigger challenges? Will you find new strength, aptitude and confidence that you didn't know you could possess? Will you be pleased or regretful with the roads you took?

There will be thousands of forks along the way, you can be certain of that. This even applies to the very last decisions that a person makes in this life. Should I keep on fighting or move on?

I know you will not always make the right choices. Nobody does. I certainly haven't. But all your choices are connected to the person you are, the person you will be. Sometimes, the truly right choice for you may be the opposite of what I would have chosen.

I'll close with a famous humorous quote from Yogi Berra, the legendary manager of the New York Yankees from the 60s. He said, "When you come to fork in the road, take it."

Take the road,
Your papi

#57 THINGS I WISH I HAD TAUGHT MY SON... AND STILL CAN
How will you address your friends?...

Facebook is OK, but it would be wise to maintain a robust address book on your computer. You shouldn't just rely on your phone for this.

Your computer has a very powerful address book built-in. Whatever you put there will migrate to your phone and to your personal Internet site. What is great about this address book is that you can add details about the person or company that you have included in your database. This will come in handy when you start meeting people who share the same first name, even the same last name. Five years from now, you may forget who the person is, but if your "notes" section is good and if you've included a picture, it will tickle your memory and you'll be able to reach out appropriately.

One good thing to consider in the notes section of the address book is where these new friends and acquaintances come from. Waxahachie? Tulsa? Ontario? Japan? Someday in the future, when traveling, you may need to access insight from their city or part of the world. I have friends throughout the country and in many other countries that can help me with info or with some other form of assistance when I call upon them.

The world will become smaller when you're in college. Your little bubble circle of friends will become a bigger bubble. The people you meet will want to help you and you will want to help them succeed.

Also, your old and new friends will change their emails and phone numbers along the way. You will change yours. When you do find out a new number or email address, return to your address book and correct the file. Finally, make sure you start to build a complete set of data of your family, your cousins, your uncles, your aunts, your grandparents, your padrinos. Perhaps your extended family may not seem as connected and relevant to you. They will as you get older and wiser.

> *I got your number,*
> *Your papi*

 #58 THINGS I WISH I HAD TAUGHT MY SON... AND STILL CAN
Don't play with fire if you're fond of your eyebrows...

One of your friends gets a great idea. "Hey let's BBQ!", and everybody starts getting the stuff ready for the cookout. One important rite of passage that I haven't passed on to you is how to make a fire for a carne asada. Maybe you've got it down from the Boy Scouts, but

I don't want to assume you do. For years, I have watched different techniques for starting the fire. Some looked like right out of a scene from *Backdraft*, complete with near-miss third degree burns. Others were uneventful, slow to ramp-up examples of responsible fire-making. I'd rather you do the latter.

Have I learned this lesson the hard way? Yes. Do I want you to learn the hard way? No. Learning to start a fire from one of your inexperienced friends is like learning how to drive from a 10-year-old video (car-racing) game aficionado. He's got great conviction, but is often misinformed.

This is what I know.

Most of the time, you will use charcoal for making your burgers or fajitas. If you're in South Texas, mesquite is readily available (I can smell it now), but it must be dry. For simplicity sake, I'm gonna stick to charcoal in this email.

First you load and scatter the charcoal in the pit. You spread it around evenly with a stick so that you can have an even temperature when all the coals are firey red.

As for the starter fluid, let me tell how not to use it. Don't spray the flammable starting fluid on the coals and immediately throw a match in there. If you do, you'll get a floooumpppppp sound and perhaps burn your eyebrows off. Even worse, your fire will seem like it's on its way, but within a few minutes the starter fluid will evaporate and the fire will sputter out. To match your missing smokey eyebrows, you'll have egg on your face too. I don't know all the science behind why it works this way, but I know I was one of those nitwits that just repeated this same action over and over, burning lots of money on starter fluid and never getting it right. Thank God for long arms and quick reflexes or I would have needed new eyebrows.

Now that we're clear on how not to do it, let me explain how I was taught. One day, the father of a semi-surrogate family who decided to feed me and house me during the college summers when I did not have a dorm (they were also the parents of my best friend), saw me risking my life to start a fire in his backyard. He always spoke Spanish and he said something like, "Hey dummy, what are you doing?" but with more colorful language. He then guided me on how to do it.

After letting the fire go out. He said, "Soak the coals with starter fluid. Be generous with it." I did. Then he said, "OK, now go inside and do something else." I did. I then came back after 10 minutes and he asked me to repeat the soaking of the charcoal briquets. I did it again. "Wait about five minutes more." I did. Then he said, "Now strike a match and throw it in." I did. And magically, the fire started slowly and then grew and grew. This time it didn't burn out in a few minutes. The fire burned steady and eventually the coals became a glowing orange.

That reminds me… You don't want to put anything on the grill until the coals are glowing orange and white. Otherwise, your meat or chicken or whatever you are grilling will taste like charcoal (yucky). This white orangey firey color will also coincide with the fire being hot enough to cook the meat. Be aware that meat and chicken and sausage let off juices that sometimes drip and cause fire to shoot up when those juices combine with oxygen. If it looks like the flames are damaging the meat, just close the top of the grill and the flames will die down. Meanwhile, the heat will build up, cooking the meat evenly.

I am by no means an expert at cooking on a grill and I have made my fair share of nasty-tasting food. I'm sure I'll get corrected on my technique in the future but at least these tips will keep you from getting burned and ruining meat.

Is it done yet?
Your papi

 #59 THINGS I WISH I HAD TAUGHT MY SON… AND STILL CAN
Don't wait for somebody else to do it…

Sometimes you stand by and do nothing or strategically look away. Maybe you start a conversation or pretend to look busy. Meanwhile, somebody is struggling a few feet away. He or she is putting away chairs, lugging heavy equipment, picking up trash… The person is doing something tedious or strenuous and you just look on but never lift a finger, lend a hand.

There are two kinds of people when it comes to these situations. There are those who don't ever get that mental click that tells them they should help. They think that they are above this type of menial, "low-life" work. They may even joke about how nobody is helping the "grunt". Then there are those who scan (not always but often) for an opportunity to help. They don't wait to be asked, they just do it. They don't have the "it's not my job" syndrome. They don't approach it from the "what's in it for me?" angle. That's just the way they are.

A friend of mine has four boys. I remember that whenever these boys arrived at our house for a party or when they showed up at a fund-raising function, they came to me or to anybody in charge and asked how they could be of assistance. Sometimes they just got to work. These were young boys ranging from ages 9 to 16. Their father was and is the same way. This orientation towards helping others is not a DNA thing, it is something learned because ultimately, this type of behavior is what keeps the world going 'round.

You can usually spot these moments of opportunity by simply asking yourself, "What's wrong with this picture?" when dozens of people completely miss the lone invisible worker (regardless of whether that person is paid or volunteering) scurrying about all around them.

I think parents want their kids to grow up learning this lesson but somehow they never verbalize it and it never gets transferred. Years pass. Then it stings when you're the parent of that child and he or she never notices the sacrifices you have made for him or her. Instead of lifting the yoke off his mom's back, he or she adds to it. Ouch!

Recalling the email I sent you about the law of reciprocity, I can almost remember every little gesture of kindness that has been sent my way. I may not remember the actual act that was done for me, but my unconscious mind remembers why I'm fond of the person who helped me with my burden.

Some parents may teach that you should never stoop to help those of lesser (supposed) status than you. I say phooey to them. Most of these folks usually see the fault in this type of thinking when wisdom finally arrives. Sometimes their eyes are opened when the very people they devalued before (and never helped) now come to their aid.

Just do it,
Your papi

 #60 THINGS I WISH I HAD TAUGHT MY SON... AND STILL CAN
The list goes on...

Mom and pop stores usually take it at the end of the year. Larger stores are computerized so they can keep track of it on a minute-by-minute basis. What is it? The "it" is their inventory. The inventory that they have is all the stuff they can sell. Have you taken inventory of how blessed you are?

I have. And I do all the time.

I am blessed to be loved by my wife. I am blessed to be loved by my kids. I am blessed to be loved by my natural brothers and sisters. I am blessed to be loved by my brothers in Christ. I am blessed with a loving father and loving in-laws. I am blessed to have wonderful friends and I have many more to meet. I am blessed with good health. I am blessed to have abundant time to accomplish the things I want to accomplish and to have time left to be the papi I want to be. Other things that I am blessed with: A creative mind, a technical mind, a curious mind, a healthy appetite, enough stamina to stay semi-fit, enough focused concentration to organize abstract ideas, an understanding of music composition, and the list goes on for several hours...

The word inventory comes from the Latin word inventarium, a list of what is found. What can you find?

It's very easy to focus on the things we don't have. It's the American way, I guess. Distracted by what we don't have, we tend to overlook the thousands of things that we have been blessed with. Onlookers from other countries can't believe how plush our lives are. And they can't help but notice how we take for granted our abundance.

Therefore…

Take inventory of how blessed you are every day. In other words, be thankful for all the straightforward blessings, even the mixed blessings. Be mindful of the setbacks and appreciate the learning opportunity they can become for you.

It sounds cliché to tell you to be grateful for your ability to eat, sleep, walk, talk, read, write, listen and live pain free.

But on this very day, I know somebody who just had her gums and teeth removed due to cancer, she can't eat or speak. I know people who can't sleep, and haven't been able to rest peacefully in a long time. My father can walk, but he would love to be able to run and jump around like you. Several friends are learning how to talk again after a stroke. A friend named Jesus has such bad dyslexia that letter combinations and words don't mean anything to him. Migraines plague another friend and listening to anything is a monumental task. And I can name at least a hundred people (close friends) in some kind of pain right now.

> *Count your blessings… 1, 2, 3, 4,∞,*
> *Your papi*

 #61 THINGS I WISH I HAD TAUGHT MY SON… AND STILL CAN
Endurance is…

I just finished reading *50/50*, the second book by Dean Karnazes. In his first book, *Ultramarathon Man*, Dean writes about how on his 30th birthday he gets the itch to run. He runs home from a bar where he had been celebrating, his typical go-nowhere drinking buddy routine. But he's not satisfied with his run home. So instead of going inside and waking his wife or daughter, he strips down to his boxer shorts and undershirt, grabs some old sneakers he finds in his garage and heads out running into the night. He doesn't stop until he is 30 miles from home. Later in the book, he finds out about The Western States 100, a 100-mile race that traverses a few mountains. He completes that successfully (the way he describes it is fascinating). Not satisfied with that he completes a 120-mile run in 120-degree weather in Death Valley. Not satisfied with that he runs 15 miles in the arctic South Pole and when he gets to the pole, he runs around it a few times. Yes… This guy is a maniac. He ends his book with an insane non-stop 220-mile run. When he finishes, he has energy left over to take his daughter to an amusement park. Crazy!

In his second book, Dean Karnazes runs 50 (26.2 miles) marathons in 50 days (consecutively) in 50 states (including Alaska and Hawaii). I listened (it was an audio book) in disbelief. I thought about my inability to run a mile without collapsing. One note that stood out among all the other amazing points he makes is that once the body gives up, the spirit can take over, allowing the person to go further than he or she has ever gone before.

Is he different from me? He says in his book that he's not. And if he isn't, then why do I give up so quickly when I hit the road running.

Tonight I am writing from Dallas. I drove up here today for the opening of a friend's new company. On the way I finished *50/50* just 50 miles shy of Fort Worth. I looked over to the right and saw some picturesque rolling hills dotted with cows along a winding road. I had the time. Heck, why not? Even though I hate to run, I parked the van, changed into running shorts and started running with my new found inspiration. Last night I ran a mile and got completely exhausted. Today I ran two miles. I wanted to find that spirit that shows up to take you the extra mile. Maybe on the way back, I'll find another interesting setting and perhaps go an extra mile. I don't remember the last time I ran two miles non-stop, I would guess at least 15 years ago.

Endurance is not just a running thing. The word, endurance, comes from in (in) durus (hard), to make hard. Endurance means to keep on keeping on. It is sticking to whatever you're doing until you cross the finish line, be it physical or mental. In your world, the next finish line is graduating from college. But there will be more journeys requiring hard-fought endurance. Your relationships, be they friendship or spousal, will last from the same spirit that drives you to complete a marathon. Even if running is not your thing, I'm not sure it's mine, you will get more out of life if you strive for something big… And stick with it 'til you hear your preferred soundtrack music playing (in the background) at the end of your long hard-fought battle.

> *Gotta run now,*
> *Your papi*

 #62 THINGS I WISH I HAD TAUGHT MY SON… AND STILL CAN
The temple…

So I'm driving back from Dallas and I hit a traffic jam in Temple, Texas. It looks like a long one so I get on the access road and spot a sign that says, Lake Belton five miles. I've never seen

Lake Belton. I head in its direction since it is a better option than sitting in the IH-35 parking lot. When I arrive there, I am treated to a beautiful and very clean lake.

There is a passage in 1 Corinthians, chapter 6 that talks about how to treat our bodies. Paul (the writer of this letter) advises that our bodies are our temples. Over the years I've heard that term of the body as a temple by different presenters and experts. One group that I've heard use this temple metaphor is the holistic advocates. They propose that we put natural, organic, good-for-you food in your body, your temple. I'll elaborate on what these are later. Others who have jumped on the bandwagon using this same symbolism are the exercise and fitness industry. Exercise is how you take care of the temple, they say. Finally, the anti-drug, anti-smoking, and anti-alcohol groups advocate that you should not defile your temple with these harmful chemicals and carcinogens.

I pretty much agree with them all.

So I thought it apropos that when in Temple, do something for my temple. Before me was this gorgeous lake and hardly anyone enjoying it. So I marked out my path, pulled out my jogging shoes, changed into running shorts and went the extra mile. Still on my high from Dean Karnazes book, I ran just a little over three miles. I smiled throughout my run not knowing whether I was happy or wincing. Your friend Daniel's mom is running 13 miles (a half marathon) in a few weeks. Before this year, she had never been a runner. A few blocks from her house is my friend Fred and his wife Leslie who will both be running 26.2 miles to complete a marathon. They've been training all year for this. Their temples are probably sparkling.

The lesson for today is to consider how you take care of your temple. From eating right to staying fit (I know you are very fit now, but so was I when I was a freshman in college), and staying as far away from destructive behaviors as you can. Beer companies will be dropping billions of dollars trying to get you to defile your temple. Tobacco companies will do the same. You and your friends represent the most sought after group of consumers (prey) that these temple-destroying companies want to add to their statistics. To them, you are not a human. You are volume. You are sales. They literally want to crash your life party.

Every man is the builder of a temple called his body. — *Henry David Thoreau (1817-1862)*

> *Take care of your temple,*
> *Your papi*

✉ #63 THINGS I WISH I HAD TAUGHT MY SON... AND STILL CAN
Independence...

It was an unforgettable Fourth of July. Between the southside of Dallas and Fort Worth is Joe Pool Lake. You (two-years-old at the time), your sister (four-month-old) your mom, several friends and myself planned a day outing at the park area of this lake. The place was swarming with people all with the same idea, to have a good time. Mostly we just sat around in the shade and made food on a little grill. People were swimming in the lake but I didn't like the muddy color of the water. There was a stage with a band and lots of loud music. We were laughing and joking. We went to the playground. You played with Yuri and Cristal. Everything was nice.

Then you weren't there.

I looked out and saw thousands of people and I couldn't believe they were still having a good time while your mother and I were in panicked-anguish. I immediately ran towards the water dreading the worst. Between all the swimmers, I looked for any abnormal movements on the surface of the water. I turned back and saw your mother running towards the bandstand. I ran along the edge of the water trying to find any sign of you. I saw my friends running every which way around the park grounds. Everybody else just went along with their day with no worries. I saw your mother run-walking with a park ranger towards the location where we last saw you. She had a helpless look of pain on her face.

Time stood still. It was a nightmare in broad daylight.

Meanwhile about 100 yards away, you were crying between two parked cars, scared, paralyzed. Thank God somebody arriving at the park at just that moment noticed you crying. You were brought to us, and our young family was reunited.

The lesson for today is the same lesson I've been teaching you and your siblings for some time. We are connected. Your actions, your decisions, your successes and failures are connected to us, your family. What may seem to you like an independent and isolated decision is actually just one domino in a series of other dominoes that either have a positive or negative ripple effect on all of us.

When you were two, your curiosity led you to wander off. You're a young man now. Making independent decisions with lasting consequences will present themselves more frequently. If you wander off again and lose your way, know that our love is unconditional.

> *Wander safely,*
> *Your papi*

#64 THINGS I WISH I HAD TAUGHT MY SON... AND STILL CAN
ATM (Automatic Take your Money machine)

Last week I heard that the average cost for an out-of-network ATM fee has gone up to $3.43. Ouch! I'll write that again. Ouch! This is a charge that is completely avoidable but people still rationalize that it is just a couple of bucks or three and approve the charge.

Paying this amount to withdraw $40 from an ATM is like paying 9% interest. Paying $3.50 to get $20 out is like paying 18% interest to get your money. Making one withdrawal a week with these new out-of-network fees would roughly cost $180 a year. I would love to hold people's money and then charge them 18% to give it back to them in increments, but people would say that I'm mean. Go figure.

I wrote early on about how banks will be preying on you for bounced checks. They will call their fees "courtesy" but there's nothing courteous about them. Banks are especially hurting right now and they want to share the hurt or transfer it completely to you if they can. They're trying to add bogus monthly fee credit reports. They want to get you hooked on paperless (online) statements and then they remove them so that you'll pay later to get your statement when you have to contest a charge. This can be avoided if you make a PDF of the statement and keep them in a folder named bank statements. Credit reports, you don't need every month.

Don't throw money away at out-of-network bank ATMs. Plan accordingly and avoid the avoidable setbacks. Remember to get daily messages on your balance by email. Question questionable fees on your statement.

No more bank cha chings!

Your papi

 #65 THINGS I WISH I HAD TAUGHT MY SON... AND STILL CAN
Old dog... New tricks... Or old tricks in a new way

Mijo... I don't know if you've noticed but I haven't sent a lesson that doesn't apply to me also. While I may have learned some of these lessons along the way, I need to refresh my commitment to them too. Routine, while a good thing in many situations, can also desensitize us from why we should follow certain guides and behaviors.

This project has allowed me to take inventory of whether I have traveled along my journey skipping or tripping along the way. I am trying to include the lessons I wish I had learned earlier. Whether you decide to climb a corporate ladder, trek across Africa or take a deep dive into some other field of interest, most of these lessons will still apply… Perhaps even more as you get older.

So what is the lesson for today? The lesson for today is that these "things" are not just for young 20-somethings, they are even for us 40-somethings and 50-somethings and 60-somethings. Learning is a lifetime achievement endeavor. Many people who thought that they had learned all they needed to know got a cold-bucket-of-water awakening when the computer revolution happened to them. Now they're busy learning how to Google and download and burn and click and text and fetch…

Bark bark woof woof,
Your papi

 #66 THINGS I WISH I HAD TAUGHT MY SON… AND STILL CAN
Here fishy, fishy, phishy…

This morning, actually a few minutes ago, I got an email from Service Credit Union. It looked pretty official, complete with company logo.

It warned me that someone has used my account from a different location. They continue with their legitimate-sounding email stating that they are opening an investigation. They then request that I confirm my banking details so that they can safeguard my account. Sounds phishy.

So that it will be convenient for them to rob me of my identity or my bank account, they ask me to click the link they sent along in their html email. They state that if I do not respond within 48 hours, they will close my account. These hacker jerks continue with their deception by informing me that they are just trying to ensure that my bank account is not being used fraudulently.

Only one problem… I don't have a Service Credit Union account. Secondly, no bank or other type of financial institution would send this type of email to investigate fraud. They would call.

The term used for this type of fraud is "Phishing". It is an attempt to acquire sensitive information like user names, passwords, credit card details and other identity information through the use of an official sounding masquerade. It sounds legitimate. It looks legitimate. It must be, right? No… It's something phishy.

What happens next, if you get lured into clicking on the link, is that you'll be directed to an imposter website where your personal information will be compromised and you will be ripped off.

What did I do? I went to Service Credit Union's website (I had never heard of them before today). On the front page of their site is a warning about recent phishing activities. They provide instructions to forward the fraudulent emails to them and to the government entity in charge of investigating this type of deceptive behavior.

Phishing is popular with services imitating well-known companies like YouTube, Facebook, MySpace, eBay, Yahoo and PayPal. If ever you receive an email like the one I received today, never click the link. Go to the company's official website, look for the "contact us" information and let them know about the email.

> *Don't take the bait,*
> *Your papi*

 #67 THINGS I WISH I HAD TAUGHT MY SON… AND STILL CAN
The Audacity of Hope…

I don't know if you stayed up last night watching the country respond to the news that Barack Obama would be the 44th President of the United States. I'm sure you couldn't miss it. Although we in Texas had nothing to do with the outcome of this election, it is an important moment in the history of this country.

Today, Paul and I feel a little strange. He sent me an email from Ecuador stating that *The Olé Degree* is what happened yesterday to McCain and the Republican Party. It's a bit eerie to have seen this one coming even before Obama went to Washington to become a U.S. Senator. We didn't just sit around and talk about it four years ago, though. We actually wrote a book about how it would be done. It seems that the victor's campaign manager took the play-by-play direction from the pages of our book. I know he didn't but what we wrote is an allegory of what happened. Interestingly, *The Olé Degree* story will be re-enacted in this country again and in other parts of the world, in a business context, in an economic context, in a political context, in a religious context.

Because I have spent 20 years marketing from an inter-cultural angle, I have a sixth sense for seeing things through the lenses through which "forgotten" people see them. Curves, the gym that I wrote about some time ago, made an empire from the women who felt disenfranchised by the large "just for men and hard-body women" gyms. Therefore, they culturally converged at Curves (and now it is a smashing success).

President-elect Barack Obama did the same. He was like a giant mirror (or collection of small mirrors) that reflected back the unmet needs of the most disenfranchised (shadowed) people in the country… The supposedly apathetic youth, the don't-worry-about-them-because-they-never-vote African-Americans and Latinos, the people who suffer from uninsuritis, the low income displaced whites. He even scored with the kids on Nickelodeon. People voted for their hope that they saw reflecting off of him. Early on, Obama took ownership of the context of hope and change. He even wrote a book on the subject called *The Audacity of Hope*. I would say that he succeeded. He then proceeded to build on this platform because his campaign gurus knew that the current condition of this country was not what "the other American people" wanted. For McCain to try to use this same "change" platform was like deliberately shooting himself in his own campaign's foot. He only strengthened Obama's brand architecture every time he broached the subject of change. This is what Paul Goya calls a Brandframe.

Four years ago, Bush defeated John Kerry by using the frame of "beware of the flip-flopper" (because he had changed his mind about Iraq and wasn't steadfast in his resolve). Kerry blundered when he tried to prove that he wasn't a flip-flopper because he ended up helping Bush's campaign. This insight has taken me a long time to learn. Most Americans haven't figured out how this works and fall for it easily. I don't want you to be one of them.

Mijo… I am neither Democrat nor Republican because both parties have lied through their teeth and have committed atrocities. I pray that those in leadership, including Obama, demonstrate humility as they lead us out of this complicated mess. And oh yeah… Just like my example of taking our fish "Fishy" out of her fishbowl, I know these words will one day be taken out their context and I will be framed as a un-American, unpatriotic, un-Catholic, or un-something. Then you will understand what framing is all about.

Olé,
Your papi

 #68 THINGS I WISH I HAD TAUGHT MY SON… AND STILL CAN
The power of forgiveness…

Many springs ago, when you were about nine or ten, we went to the Trinity University outdoor basketball courts to shoot around. I blocked every shot you tried to get in the hoop. No matter what you tried, nothing got past me. Ouch! So what if I was six feet one-and-a-half inches and your were a little over four feet. Needless to say, I made you cry. Your mom got after me too. Sooner or later you forgave me.

In your life, there have been many occasions when I punished you for something you did or didn't do. Perhaps you didn't get to go to a birthday party when you were a child. Perhaps you didn't get to join the sleepover at a friend's house. Perhaps you didn't get that gotta-have-thing that I refused to get for you. Sooner or later you forgave me.

I've had to do some serious forgiving throughout my life. Big broken hearts have forgiven me along the way too, your mom and my parents especially.

The act of forgiving is one of the most powerful gestures that springs from the most powerful life force, love. Forgiving someone who has wronged you is a liberating experience for the one doing the forgiving. Ironically, grudges often end up hurting the wrong person. Mental and emotional bile builds up and eats away at the person who can't forgive. Meanwhile, the person who created the original offense rarely thinks about what he or she did. I am sorry for the times I have been insensitive and inflicted pain. Today, I am a free man because I don't hold any grudges.

> *Forgive me if I have offended you,*
> *Your papi*

 #69 THINGS I WISH I HAD TAUGHT MY SON... AND STILL CAN
Lose graciously...

Your sister is heartbroken today because they lost in the state semi-finals. Lots of tears were shed, perhaps more will follow. Last year, your trek to the finals ended short prematurely. Your second youngest brother lost his city soccer championship last night. However, he weathered the outcome better than most teenagers because he still got his goody bag of candy and fun stuff.

You will win some. You will lose some. When you win, you won't need so much advise other than to remain humble while you bask in the spotlight of victory. Be kind and thoughtful to those you have defeated. However, when you lose, be in the moment and lose with a purpose. Don't lose the opportunity to reflect and learn from the lessons that accompany a hard-fought loss.

I know you will forever remember your locker room heart-to-heart after your loss at Regionals last year. You shared with me the power and honor of the gracious things that were said and the tears that were shared. Don't ever forget that losing has just as much to do with the forming of your character as winning. It will even help you appreciate winning more.

There are many contests left in your life. Perhaps they will not take the form of a sport. When the tally or score is final, you may come up short again. But know this… Some apparent losses will be wins in the long run.

It's almost the end of your first quarter,
Your papi

 #70 THINGS I WISH I HAD TAUGHT MY SON… AND STILL CAN
The dead fish…

I used to have a boss that moved from New York City to San Antonio. He was a crazy eccentric Cuban. He did everything intensely, including the passing on of his "how to succeed in business" lessons. When he met me I shook his hand. He said, "What's this?" I responded, "What's what?" Still holding my hand he said, "this". "I'm shaking your hand." Then he informed me that I don't know how to shake a hand. "This is not a hand shake! This is a dead fish. You're giving me a dead fish." He then taught me how to properly shake a hand, American business style, military style. It had to be firm he said. Otherwise, I would be judged prematurely as submissive by the person on the other side of the arm. It took me quite a long time to get rid of my fish handshake. I sorta didn't care too much about it.

Boy did it come in handy (pun intended) when I won the Army account. It seemed that every soldier from private to General expected a stiff handshake (I think they go to handshake school). Thankfully, the dead fish was a thing of the past. I did ok.

The lesson for today is to pay attention to your handshake. While you may not care too much about how you do the shake, you may start off on the wrong foot when a handshake connoisseur who holds a very strong bias against dead fish judges you wrongly. It may matter when you seek some help or respect from this person.

Get a grip… A good grip,
Your papi

 #71 THINGS I WISH I HAD TAUGHT MY SON… AND STILL CAN
Look into their eyes.

In tandem with a firm handshake that I wrote about in the last email is the conscious act of looking a person in the eye(s). Let's say you are having a meeting with a professor or an employer… Not being able to connect eyes every once in a while during the conversation can send an unintended and usually unwanted message. It may suggest that you are bored, rude, uncomfortable, uninterested, afraid, lacking in self-esteem and a whole litany of other undesirable messages.

I have to admit that I had to learn to look a person in the eye. My eyes were heavy and switchy (I don't know if switchy is a word but it is now). I looked nervous which made me nervous because I knew that I looked nervous. I was a mess. Sometimes I rationalized my downturned gaze to my knowing that I was an introvert. Sometimes, I used personal insight as a crutch to match my perfectly fitting shy mask. I wasted so much time donning that stupid mask.

Eye contact is important to teachers, employers, co-workers, girls, children, classroom audiences, etc. An employer who doesn't get a right read from you can wrongly assume that you're hiding something because you can't look up. Meanwhile, everything you have worked for, prepared for, studied for, dissolves right before your very eyes because those same flighty eyes never come unglued from that chair or that floor that you're so adamantly focused on.

If every neuron in your brain is telling you that you can't do it, they're liars. Those betraying neurons can be re-programmed to feel super comfortable while engaged in an eye to eye conversation. Practice looking at yourself in the mirror, aiming your glance correctly. When looking at the person you are dialoguing with, it may help to look at just one eye, the left eye is a good one. Looking at both eyes feels a bit weird. Your ultimate intent is to have a pleasant conversation even if it feels awkward to you.

The bottom line is that you have to learn this lesson or it will haunt you. You'll wake up in a cold sweat with eyeballs dangling from the ceiling (just kidding). But seriously, repetition will eventually make this conscious effort into something as natural as breathing. It can be done. You can do it. And then you can tell others how you got over it. Maybe you'll tell your son how to do the same.

> *Here's looking at you kid,*
> *Your papi*

 #72 THINGS I WISH I HAD TAUGHT MY SON... AND STILL CAN
Happy cries.

I was going to write about something else, but I got a note from Lisa, one of the readers of *Things I Wish I Had Taught My Son... And Still Can*. And I had a happy cry. And I remember now how much I love to experience happy cries.

By the way… Real men know how to cry.

I remember one day putting a CD on the stereo in our living room of a song I felt expressed my love for my wife, your mom. The name of the song is *"My Heart Belongs to You"*. I held mami in my arms and sang her this song while we looked into each other's eyes. Happy tears followed from both of us. Not paying attention to what was occurring at our legs, we looked down and saw your third little sister (about four at the time) looking up. She was crying too. With tears still in my eyes, I asked, "Why are you crying mija?" Logically she answered, "Because mami and papi are crying."

"But we're crying because mami and papi are happy," mami said trying to explain this irrational concept to your little hermanita. With all the composure she could muster your little sis then said, "Well… then I'm happy too," and dissolves into uncontrollable crying… A truly special moment.

Watch this video… It will bring happy tears to your eyes:
http://www.youtube.com/watch?v=MslbhDZoniY&feature=related

Happy tears are healing. They wash you of all the unsettled stuff inside. They nurture you. They water you like a plant. They make your day.

I'll share one more happy tears moment. Your oldest sister had a very high fever when she was about six or seven. Mom was off on a retreat and I was doing my best to console your little ill sister. She couldn't even open her eyes. She just lay limp on her bed suffering. Sitting on the edge of her bed and in an attempt to get her mind off the fever, I asked her to sing to me. She didn't think about it for a split second… She just started singing in a very fragile voice… "The sun'll come out tomorrow, bet your bottom dollar that tomorrow… there'll be sun!," the song from *Annie*.

> *Guess what I was doing?*
> *Your papi*

 #73 THINGS I WISH I HAD TAUGHT MY SON… AND STILL CAN
Wanna-do(s), gotta-do(s), almost dues and overdues…

There are things piling up that you need to get to. However, if they're not on a list, organized and readily accessible, these things (swimming around in your head) are just taking up valuable concentration time (every time you think about them) from you and still not getting done.

Your email program has a To Do function built-in. You can list all the things you need to take care of in this convenient remind-you list. When you add an item in the To-Do section of your email program, it automatically shows up in the calendar application. They work in tandem to keep you organized. If you add the to-do list in the calendar, it will automatically show up in the email program. That's pretty cool.

The next thing that will help is to set a due date for when you plan to complete that "thing". For example… All your quizzes, tests, reading assignments, papers, writing assignments, etc… should be listed here with a corresponding due date. The next important step that will help you immensely is to set up an "alarm" reminder. If you look at the to-do entry that you added on the calendar application, you can set up an alarm reminder that will send you an SMS text or an email (at the appropriate time you designate, usually with enough time to get the task done) depending on your preference. NOTE: These to-dos only work if you also itemize the in-between steps that will be needed to complete your projects on-time and satisfactorily.

When you complete the to-do item, return to the entry (in your email or calendar app) and check it off as completed so it won't show up anymore as something you gotta-do. Consider a personal project to-do list, which includes things like washing your clothes and registering for next semester. Another project may include to-do lists for each class. A to-do list makes sense for any and all responsibilities that you need to remember to do in this new life experience called college. The bottom line is this, if it takes up thinking time to keep track of it, get it out of your mind by putting it down in a centralized list, and then do it at the designated time. You'll need your concentration to remember more important things. Instead, have your computer summon you when the next to-do step of that project is due.

If you don't do this, you may think that you are free to mill around and hang out when the overdue police is around the corner. You'll be blindsided and nobody but yourself will be to blame for the negligence. Sure, it will be sobering to see what you've got to get done, but it will be more stressful to not know what angry obnoxious monster project lurks in the shadows of your disorganization because you didn't plan for it accordingly… And these monsters are not nice.

Two nights ago, I asked you to call mom. That was a to-do. You forgot. Perhaps you should have a to-do to call home every Tuesday or Wednesday at 4 PM or 6 PM when you're not in class and just walking back to your dorm.

> *I'll check off my to-do for today,*
> *Your papi*

#74 THINGS I WISH I HAD TAUGHT MY SON... AND STILL CAN
Get your head in the clouds...

People don't look up very much anymore. They're so GPSy on getting to their destination that the thought of looking up, straight up, high up, is a rare occurrence.

Today, there are some amazing clouds overhead. They are a ripply collection of rolling cotton wands with a uniform patch of deep blue between them going as far as the eye can see east and west. I can get lost in these clouds. I can find ideas in these clouds. I can find peace in these clouds.

During my time at the University of Texas, I used to walk a lot like you do. I used to find a shady place to lie down (with a clear view of the clouds) and just get lost... Imagining, reflecting, resetting.

College is a great time to get acquainted with your Stratus, Cumulus and Cirrus friends in the sky. It would be a pity to miss out on these wonderful God canvases that are painted for you and which will never look the same again. The lesson for today is: Look up.

Of course, you don't want to have your head in the clouds during class (that's a totally different concept). Also, don't be so worried about finding hidden famous people, dinosaurs or writing formations. Just lose yourself in the beauty of creation.

I wrote this short email over the course of 30 minutes.

I stopped to look at the clouds while I wrote.

> *You can say this is a cloudy thought,*
> *Your papi*

 #75 THINGS I WISH I HAD TAUGHT MY SON... AND STILL CAN
Won't power... Meet will power.

About 15 years ago, Jorge Luna, aka George Moon, gave me a book called *Life 101*. It was a life lessons book similar to the teachings I'm sending you. Thankfully, most of the wisdom in the book I took to heart but I wouldn't know this until I re-ordered and re-read the book (I lost it in some put away box or passed it along). One of the concepts in the book that I know I was impressed by was the lesson on will power and won't power.

Will power, as you may have already learned is the gumption and resolve to stay on plan... The will to follow-through with a mission. Will power is what a dieter tries to summon when a piece of cheesecake with a plop of whipped-cream on top beckons. Will power is what stays up with you at night studying when your eyelids have already gone on strike and your yawns are coming in waves.

Will power is you-can-do-it-ness.

So what is won't power.

Many people are won't-aholics… They believe that things won't work out and actually predestine their predictions to come true because they have a strong sense of won't power. They booby-trap their own progress with this overwhelming negative funk. They are cousins to the "I canters" who give up before they get started because they know they can't. This self-defeat-est orientation to life is merciless. Years go by. Opportunities go by. Life goes by. Won't power sucks all happiness away.

Whenever you feel a little won't power creeping up on you, oppositize it (made-up word). In other words, flip the language. "I won't do good on this test" can be oppositized into "I will do great on this test because I'm prepared." Fear can be flipped into excitement. Stubbornness can be flipped into determination. Oppositizing is replacing a negative, energy-drawing "I won't" thought into positive, confidence-building "I will" life fuel.

I won't get sick = I will keep my mind, body and emotions healthy… That's oppositizing.

> I _will_ hit send now,
> Your papi

 #76 THINGS I WISH I HAD TAUGHT MY SON… AND STILL CAN
The when-no-one's-lookin' version of you…

There's the you that your friends and family know and then there's the you that nobody knows. Often, people go through life managing these two you(s). The social version of themselves may be fun-loving, outgoing, generous, thoughtful, and a long list of other favorable attributes. When no one is looking though the same person may be slightly different. He or she may be judgmental, favor a dark personality, explore taboos, live a life he or she would rather not want to be known for.

About 20 years ago, a concept called WYSIWIG was introduced to the computer world. WYSIWIG stands for What You See Is What You Get. The problem with computers back then was that the screen didn't match the dot matrix and early laser printouts that used to be the only option for printing. You worked on a document, formatted it, sized it and after you printed it, the result looked vastly different from your expectations. WYSIWIG is hardly ever mentioned anymore because computers have come a long way.

However, computers have also made us, the humans, less WYSIWIG (what you see is what you get) because they have introduced us to the dark side of cyber-humanity. From secret identities to new forms of mental addictions the stakes have gone up. Today, the lure, the amount and the availability of deceptive and destructive de-humanizing input is beyond something that can be quantified. Everyday you have to walk through a mine field of the mind that doesn't get any safer when you go to sleep... Sometimes the thoughts and imagery amplify in dreams. At the end of the day, we become numb to the onslaught of this stuff... We become less human.

The lesson for today is to try to reconcile the you everybody loves with the when-no-one's-lookin' you. It's hard to have a division within yourself. At some point every single person has to manage these two opposing inner forces. Still, you have the choice to nurture the one that will make you happy for the long haul... The one that will make you whole again.

No one's lookin'... Who are you?
Your papi

 #77 THINGS I WISH I HAD TAUGHT MY SON... AND STILL CAN
Sweeping it under the carpet... or rug.

When I was a young boy in Hebbronville, the street in front of our house was unpaved. Every car that passed by our dusty caliche street sent clouds of dust toward our house, through the screens and onto our floors and furniture. Coupled with dirty work boots and muddy play shoes, the dirt piled up. Sweeping and dusting was a daily or semi-weekly event depending upon the wind. I hated to do it and my mom wanted it done quite frequently. When it was my turn to do the sweeping and when I knew that nobody was looking, I often swept the dirt into unseen corners and under furniture... I'm sure I swept stuff under the carpet a few times too.

Sweeping under the rug or under the carpet has become a metaphor for concealing, suppressing, keeping quiet, withholding information, covering up. I have had many employees sweep stuff under the rug or carpet in hopes that no one would notice an error, a shortcoming, a falsehood. Sometimes the stuff was so extensive that people tripped over the rug. Sometimes the entire company tripped over the rug. Currently, this country is tripping over the rug from all the deceptive financial practices that have been left piling up in some corner of the economy.

The lesson for today is that most of the stuff swept under the world's rug can be traced back to the sweeper. My friends who are school custodians tell me of the all the gum they find stuck under desks. They have a yearly gum removal event. Yes, if they wanted to, they could trace each gum to its chewer. The DNA trapped in each of these nasty sticky globs can probably be linked to the chewer. Imagine getting chewed out by your teacher 10 years later for that one. And I'm not even going to talk about boogers.

Anything digital and financial that is swept under the rug will certainly be uncovered with time. Lies, half-truths, stretched truths and other flavors of misrepresented truths will come back to stain your character if you were the sweeper. Perhaps, that is why people say that they've got the "dirt" on someone when they want to threaten that person.

Today's lesson is simple. If you make a mistake, own up to it. Don't sweep it under the rug and let it pile up until it gets uncovered. Chances are it will be uncovered and it won't smell good after time has passed. Don't think that it won't show up in the wash (a different metaphor for being found out) either. I know you stuffed candy wrappers in the sofa when you were younger. You stuffed several foreign objects in the VCR, too. You wouldn't admit it but a simple fingerprint analysis or DNA test could have solved the case easily.

Kinda gives new meaning to the Rugrats,
Your papi

 #78 THINGS I WISH I HAD TAUGHT MY SON... AND STILL CAN
Your song took the stage...

Last night, a combination of 12 high-school and college-aged kids were singing on a stage at the Carver Theatre. They were performing during a Christian concert. I helped them set up the audio equipment and do a sound check. I had planned to play along with them but they were set so I hung out at the back with the mixing audio engineer. This is the first time that I had helped out with a serious 36 track mixing board. All the voices, the amps, the drums, the guitars, the bass were routed to the large mixing board at the back of the theatre. It sounded really good and got better as they played on.

Three years prior, you and I were driving to your Boy Scout summer camp. I asked you to help me write a song while we went up IH-10. I had a working melody and some beginning lyrics. During the course of the ride through the Hill Country, we knocked out *"I Want To Be"*. We debated over whether people would actually sing a nonsensical pa pa ra pa pa little break in the middle of the song. You thought it was tacky and that you had a handle on what teenagers like and dislike. You predicted it would bomb. Still you helped me finish the song. Your sister helped me record it and a few weeks later about 100 teenagers were singing it at the top of their lungs, nonsensically. One of the teens used the pa pa ra pa pas to break out into an impromptu rap, which worked seamlessly.

That same song was played last night. I wasn't playing it, the teens up on the stage were playing and singing it. Half of them knew it from memory. I don't even know it by memory and you probably don't remember any of it. It was a very nice moment. I thought of our trip... And of the message of the song.

We never really know how far an idea will go. Ideas have their own lives and often they want to survive... Almost as if they have a life of their own. One of the guys from last night, J.J., a drummer and guitar player who really likes the *"I Want To Be"* song will be taking it with him to the Navy. Perhaps somebody else will find it touching or catchy or both. Perhaps a congregation across the ocean somewhere will find it appropriate for their service. I have submitted the song to a publishing company and they have a broad reach around the world. Or it may just stay in its potential state forever... And never go beyond the periphery of Northwest San Antonio.

The lesson for today is to follow your love for songwriting and to turn down your inner critic to zero. Songwriting is something you can do until death. I know you enjoy songwriting but you may tend to repress it for fear of ridicule or other too-cool-to-write reasons.

Nevertheless, poetry and songwriting are life-giving habits to pursue. They change you. They inspire you and others. They make you feel like life is in stereo.

> *Now go and compose,*
> *Your papi*

> To hear the song we wrote together, go to the following link:
> http://thingsiwishihadtaughtmyson.com/Iwanttobe.htm

 #79 THINGS I WISH I HAD TAUGHT MY SON... AND STILL CAN
Somebody's gotta do it...

I used to have a cushy job when I was a freshman in college. Because I was diligent and poked around the financial aid office of the college for weeks, I eventually landed a job at the LJC gym that worked out with my school schedule.

Every weekday, I swept the massive complex. It included the gym, the weight room, the halls, the foyer, and the men's dressing room. Once a week I had to buff the floors with a bulky machine. Three times a week, I had to scrub the two bays of showers with eight showers each. And everyday, I had to clean 18 toilets on the men's side of the gym. I won't use any adjectives to describe this task.

But considering that Laredo was usually 105 degrees hot (and it usually felt hotter than that), I had a cushy job. The other work-studies were cooking or sweeping outdoors.

When I was a freshmen in high school, I really wanted a stereo. I wanted one of those fancy new-fangled stereos that had a record player, an AM-FM radio, a cassette player (new technology) and the Holy Grail, an eight-track player. I had already picked it out at Dillard's. The only problem was the price. It was $400. And I had about $16 to my name. During summers in Hebbronville, there was really only one place you could make $400 in three weeks if you were a kid. It was picking watermelons. It was a nice stereo.

Rogelio Ibanez would pick me up in the morning. I would jump into the back of his 2.5 ton truck with tall wooden hand-made walls. This is the size of an Army truck you often see on freeways. During this particular summer we rode out to La Gloria, Texas, about an hour away. We would arrive and then form a throwing line while the truck followed several planting rows away. The strongest guy would pick up the watermelon from the dirt (back-breaking job) and throw it to the next guy on the chain. Everybody would throw these juicy striped watermelons about five or six feet to the next guy. Then the last guy would heave the watermelon up about 8.5 feet to the catcher on the truck. These two were the strongest guys in our crew. Inside, two stackers neatly fit as many watermelons as the truck could hold. We dreaded the overgrown monster watermelons. All the while, our bosses warned us of rattlesnakes, a common inhabitant of the area and dehydration. We all wore long sleeve cotton shirts, long pants, boots and bandanas in 105 degree weather. We would ride back to town on top of the watermelons and unload them onto conveyor belts. From there, another crew neatly stacked them in 18-wheelers for their trip to grocery stores and eventually picnics around the country. Meanwhile, we went back for a second load each day to repeat the ordeal a second time. I was on my way to getting that awesome stereo and little biceps were showing up on my arms.

After about three weeks of work, and after an additional four days of rain with no work and no pay, Rogelio picked me up along with the rest of the crew. We would risk it. That day we went out, loaded the truck and as we were about to leave the field, the truck eerily sank into the soft red earth. Guess what? We had to unload the truck. After we pushed the 2.5 ton truck out of the hole we had to reload it. This time we had to throw the watermelons even further. It killed me. I was wiped out for days but I had the money to get the stereo. And I think I loved the stereo so much because I understood how much it cost me.

These two jobs among many others I held, were important for my development. They all represent mini-episodes of my life. Work, jobs, careers, they help define you. I don't regret cleaning toilets… That's part of my story.

When your break for the holidays comes around, I'll need you to work to help us juggle the extra balls and watermelons we have in the air. And now that you've gotten past the first semester hump, I'll need you to find a place to work on campus. It'll help define you.

> *Now get back to work,*
> *Your papi*

PS: Your mom worked long hours for three years at Chick-fil-A starting the summer of her freshman year in college.

 #80 THINGS I WISH I HAD TAUGHT MY SON… AND STILL CAN
The language of the www…

The prevailing language that makes the Internet function is HTML. It stands for Hyper Text Markup Language. A web page created with HTML will usually have .html at the end of its name. This is similar to the concept where a Microsoft Word file ends in .doc. In your browser (usually Safari or Firefox in your case and Explorer when you're not using an Apple computer), the top blank at the top of the browser screen is the place where you type in the URL (Uniform Resource Locator) if you know it. This is where you type in yahoo.com, google.com or wikipedia.org, or dogpile.com. For this to work you need to know the URL (the Internet's term for address).

The http:// at the beginning of a web address is usually what precedes the domain name (the official and standard name of the site you are visiting). For the last few years, the Internet has been functioning properly without the http:// prefix. HTTP stands for Hyper Text Transfer Protocol which means that this is simply the Internet's delivery vehicle for getting people to their desired website. Hyper Text Markup Language (html) is delivered by the Hyper Text Transfer Protocol (http). If you look at your browser's URL address space, the long series of characters and slashes, you'll notice that it usually has an .html letter combination somewhere in its address. This doesn't apply to giant sites (Facebook.com, yahoo.com, etc) that use a different scripting language and databases to run their sites. I won't get into Flash sites for now either as this is just a 101.

There are also two main types of emails that people receive (at least I think that there are only two): text emails and HTML (there it is again) emails. Text emails only use text characters while html emails can send hyperlinks (those are the blue underlined links that save you the time of typing or cutting and pasting an address) that you can just click to arrive at a web destination. HTML emails can also display stuff that lives on a website somewhere else. They can even display an entire site within the body of an email. While it feels like the website (or music, or video) is actually in the body of the email it is only a distant mirror that is referencing the site at the very moment that you are reading your email. If your computer has no Internet connection, no information will be displayed.

The last thing I wanted to cover was how servers that host HTML websites work. Thingsiwishlhadtaughtmyson.com is a website I created to invite people to sign up to this email series. The first page on the site is actually called index.html. It lives in a folder on a computer at a company called godaddy.com. The folder (for simplicity sake) is called www.thingsiwishihadtaughtmyson.com. Because the index.html file is placed in this folder, a user who types in the web address www.thingsiwishihadtaughtmyson.com arrives at the home page of the website. Any other pages that I add to the site will be in sub-folders. Every sub-folder will be represented with a slash. Like this… /

Here's a hypothetical example: www.thingsiwishihadtaughtmyson.com/advice/myson/Internetrelated/howtomakewebsites.html is what the URL would say in your browser. In actuality, what this would mean is that there is a folder at godaddy.com called thingsiwishihadtaughtmyson.com. Within that folder is another folder called "advice". Within the "advice" folder would be another folder called "myson". Within that folder would be another folder called "Internetrelated". And within that folder would be an HTML web page called howtomakewebsites.html. Each forward slash means another sub-folder.

Eventually, everybody with a website (business or personal) will come to learn this very strange language. And they'll get a weird feeling inside when they realize that they actually understand it. I think this is how my parents or my parent's parents must have felt when they learned how to use street addresses and zip codes.

> *Dogoodinschool/takecare/begood/iloveyou.html,*
> *Your papi*

 #81 THINGS I WISH I HAD TAUGHT MY SON… AND STILL CAN
A great fish story…

I went deep-sea fishing this past summer. I was one of the only guys on the boat who didn't throw up, which means I felt queasy all day. We caught nothing in the morning and right about noon, bam, we started pulling out lots of Red Snappers from the Gulf of Mexico. We also pulled out some sharks (one was a hammerhead that got tangled… it was mine but my friend Richard took credit for it… that's the story and I'm sticking to it), a Kingfish, and a Grouper. Everybody got at least two Reds.

We've been on a few fishing trips together… White bass fishing with Joe and lake fishing several times. I can't say that I've taught you how to fish (I'm not that good), but we've brought a few in over the years.

"If you give a man a fish, you feed him for a day. If you teach a man how to fish, you feed him for a lifetime." This little Chinese proverb was spoken or written by K'ung Fu-tzu 551-479 B.C.E., better known as Confucius around these parts. Lao Tzu is also referenced as having given us these words of wisdom. I'll let Confucius and Lao figure it out.

I have not always followed these words of wisdom even though I subscribe to them. So many times, I have tried to do it alone because of the old adage, "if you want to do it right, you've gotta do it yourself." Often, I have worked myself into a corner because I didn't teach my children or associates how to do a particular something. Too many times, I just handed out fish (I know you don't like fish, but go with it).

Every Sunday after playing in the choir, I have lots of kids (five to seven-year-olds) who want to help put away the mic stands and speaker equipment. I used to shoo them away. Now I teach them how I'd like the task to be done. They're like little groupies and they're learning how to handle delicate equipment. I should have taught you more about mechanical things and computer things and cooking things. I guess I still am. I'm glad we were able to build the three connected playhouses as your Eagle Scout project. During this project, my dad and your mom's uncle were the sensei(s). They taught us both how to fish.

If you decide to put these many lessons to work for you, they will feed you for a lifetime (provided you learn to like fish). If you need my help on anything in the future, you know I will come to your assistance. However, I will be sporting my new and improved Confucius fishing hat. In other words, I won't do it for you. I will teach you how to do it for yourself.

> *Your fishing buddy,*
> *Your papi*

 #82 THINGS I WISH I HAD TAUGHT MY SON… AND STILL CAN
I won't drink to that…

Today I read about a 90-year-old Grammy winning piano player from Cuba named Bebo Valdes. He just put out a new CD entitled *Lagrimas Negras.* Throughout the article, the writer who covered the story dialogued with Bebo about his success and gift for composing and performing. At the closing of the article, the interviewer asks Bebo what the secret to his good health is. Bebo replies that if he mentioned the secret then it wouldn't be a secret any longer. "But just between you and me, I don't smoke and I don't drink," Bebo quietly stated.

Sometimes I think that the university experience is just an extended party sponsored by Budweiser. It seems that universities have violated the trust of the parents who send their children there. Perhaps they should be re-classified as "learning to drink" institutions. But then again, some parents are proud of their kid's alcohol consumption. I'm not. Unlike Bebo, I do drink, but when I do it is rare. I perhaps drink a six pack and two or three bottles of red wine per year.

I rarely think about alcohol. I don't need it to improve any situation. In a "party" situation, my lack of consumption of alcohol puts me in the position to see how much of a depressant it actually is. People really spill their guts when under the influence. Make no mistake, beer depresses you. At first it gives you the giggles, then an uncertain funk arrives and stays around.

Throughout your life, if you do partake of this American cultural pastime, you will spend thousands of dollars on these addictive and destructive beverages. I have sat across the table from men who have drunk years of their life away. I have held them as they have cried and convulsed in utter shame and regret. One day they were young and invincible. The next day they were old and miserable. They had hurt their wives, their children, their parents, their friends.

At my 25th class reunion (just a little get-together) last week, I spent most of the night talking to a friend who I hadn't spoken to since we were freshmen or sophomores in high school. He spent most of his life under the influence of some chemical even while in high school. I rejoiced when he told me and everybody else that he had found himself. All night we spoke of the hope he had for the future. He drank a Dr. Pepper and spoke of his songwriting, poetry and incredible thirst for learning. Thank God.

It cost him more than 25 years. That's a steep price to pay for an induced yet fleeting "happiness".

I'm not preaching, I'm just informing you of the unglamorous side of partying. Too many cheesy anti-drinking or anti-smoking commercials won't impact you. Perhaps I won't be able to convince you otherwise.

But know this… I love you and I pray you don't miss out on life in any way because a "friend" or "friends" introduced you to an addiction that sent you on an out-of-control spiral. I guarantee you that they won't be there to pick up the pieces.

Take it from 90-year-old Bebo… Because life is too short,
Your papi

 #83 THINGS I WISH I HAD TAUGHT MY SON… AND STILL CAN
The sequel…

Six years ago, I sifted through many of the videos that I had captured of you and your brothers and sisters. I put hundreds of short scenes of your growing-up antics into a movie woven together with storytelling music. It lasted about a half hour. I called the movie *Mis Hijos.* We've viewed it many times over the years and gifted it to relatives. And since it's been watched so much lately (probably three times a week), I've decided to start a new movie project. Currently your third youngest sister is looking for funny and heartwarming scenes to weave a story together.

There are high expectations from all your brothers and sisters on this upcoming movie. So many videos and just a blur remains in my memory bank of the years that have gone by but they are forever captured onto tape. Mom and I have been on the sidelines of your growing up years toting our cameras since the second week you were born (back then I borrowed a camera to capture your first weeks). It is fun to pull out what appears to be more than a 200-tape video history. Your youngest brother has been nagging after me to make this video because he wasn't born yet when I made the previous *Mis Hijos* movie. Now he wants to have a starring role in the sequel.

My Story, thestorytellingplace.com, my baby company, is beginning to get traction. NPR (National Public Radio) has deemed next week to be national storytelling week. If I had the correct Vújà De several years ago, I will be ready when people start to get the urge to story-tell for future generations. Two 83-year-old characters are coming to capture their story. Apparently, their daughters say that they are hams when they get to storytelling.

I look forward to weaving a new movie with your touching and funny moments in the next coming week. Perhaps on Thanksgiving Day we'll have a world premiere of *Mis Hijos II.*

Anyway… Looking forward to your coming home for the Thanksgiving weekend.

The lesson for today… Don't rely on your memory when you form a family. I don't remember 3/4s of what I've shot. Who knows if tape or portable drives will be the medium for capturing moving images, but whatever the technology, do your family a favor and movie-tize those moments. I think you'll appreciate it. Your family will too.

You oughta be in pictures,
Your papi

 #84 THINGS I WISH I HAD TAUGHT MY SON... AND STILL CAN
We were on a mission...

This morning at 7 AM, your next oldest brother, his Boy Scout troop and I departed on a hike from Mission Concepción just south of downtown. We had as a destination Mission Espada where we would take a breather and promptly turn back. According to my best estimate, each way was 7.1 miles (because of all the off-road foot-trails). Now, after the long hike, your brother and I can barely walk but we feel fully accomplished for having gone the extra miles. This is the longest trek I have ever completed. And early next year, Armando T. and I will begin training for a marathon.

Where are you on your mission?

I'm not referring to a walking trail. I'm also not so much worried with the trappings of a mission statement. You'll probably get several structured opportunities to jot down your mission statement. Actually, I have no idea where my last mission statement ended up (after several office moves) but I know that I'm living it (I'll try to dig it up). Instead, I'm interested in transferring to you the idea that some of your goals will take time (some you may forget altogether although you may unknowingly complete them). Still, many of your larger goals will seem very difficult, even impossible.

The lesson for today is to stretch your imagination and visualize what you want. Form a clear mental image of what a completed goal might look like and just try to get one step closer tomorrow. While life happens, your mission will fall into place. I like the way Paulo Coehlo puts it in *The Alchemist*, the book I asked you to read in high school... "When a person really desires something, all the universe conspires to help that person to realize his dream."

I don't know if I have the wherewithal to complete a marathon. But today's 14.2 mile hike got me one step closer to understanding what it takes. Tomorrow, when I wake up, the soreness will remind me that I did something big today (at least for me). I'll smile and go through my day knowing that I once said I would do what I did today (I tried it back in the early 90s and didn't get very far).

And I'll also smile because your brother accomplished what I couldn't get around to doing, a full 31 years ahead of schedule.

> *I hope the universe conspires to get you what you want,*
> *Your papi*

 #85 THINGS I WISH I HAD TAUGHT MY SON... AND STILL CAN
You've got connections...

Your grandmother, Marilu Castillo de Gonzalez, on your mother's side is a poet. She has a published book of poetry and probably has hundreds more stashed away. During the late 70s, that same grandma was composing music for the Latin America's songwriting equivalent of American Idol, *El OTI*. Your great grandmother, Leonarda Flores de Ramírez, on my side of the family tree (my dad's mom) was a sought after designer of one-of-a-kind quilts. We have one. She also made a hand-me-down remedy for rheumatoid arthritis from Peyote cactus, a wild hallucinogen. Her husband, Fernando Ramírez, worked in a cotton gin. You look like him. Your great grandmother (Maria Enriquez de Allen) from your mother's side (your grandmom's mom) was a famous artist and art teacher in Chicago along with her famous photographer husband (Harold Allen). She spoke no English. He spoke no Spanish, but they were madly in love with each other till the end. His works are still displayed at the Art Institute of Chicago. She received an award from the National Women's Caucus with a show in Brooklyn.

You mom's uncle, Mario Castillo, painted the first Latino mural, the first anti-Vietnam War mural and the first multicultural mural in Chicago. He has devoted his painting life to a unique form of storytelling layered Pre-Columbian art... A modern day codex of the ancient Mexican cultures. His artwork is published in several books and is displayed at the National Museum of Mexican Art in Chicago (mariocastillo.net). I also featured him and one of his giant paintings on a Coca Cola commercial in 1988.

There are lots of fascinating people in everybody's family. There are lots of fascinating people in your family too if you take the time to uncover the stories. Your 'buelito, my dad, was struck by a piece of shrapnel from the most powerful gun of World War II, an 88 millimeter anti-tank gun. He was injured as he entered the town of Bitburg, Germany. He spent almost a year in bed convalescing. Technically, he fought for this country as a Mexican citizen because his naturalization papers didn't arrive until after he was recovering in England. Through some genealogical uncovering, it turns out he was already a U.S. citizen. Your great, great, great, great, great grandfather, Don Cristobal Ramírez received a Spanish Land grant (for land north of the Rio Grande) from the King of Spain in 1767, nine years before the Declaration of Independence was signed.

I've only uncovered the tip of the story iceberg. I'm continuing to find interesting things that you and your brothers and sisters, as well as your children's children will come to value.

The lesson for today is to participate in the golden chapters of the lives of your grandparents. They may not be trendy or the kings of cool, but they connect you to history and that's cool. They add dimension to your story.

> *Their story is your story,*
> *Your papi*

 #86 THINGS I WISH I HAD TAUGHT MY SON... AND STILL CAN
Do things with modulation... Huh?

One summer day in the 70s, my cousin Oscar and I were bragging about who could eat more at Whataburger. On the menu was the grand kahuna of burgers, the triple meat, triple cheeseburger. The single is plenty large by burger standards, the triple was overkill. We also tacked on fries and completed the challenge with large chocolate milkshakes. Yowza! Our pride was much larger than our stomachs so we both ate and drank every last bite and drink of our meal. Because we ate it on the way home while in the back of a bumpy truck's camper, we got sick. We rolled around on the bed of the pickup truck holding our stomachs, miserable and on the verge of throwing up. We had too much of a good thing. We didn't moderate.

There will always be a threshold where you become disinterested in something that you liked before because it was too readily available and too frequently consumed. People can overdo it on almost anything. People can work too much. People can earn too much. People can overdose on TV or music or even health food.

Moderation is one of those of adult words that seems to bounce off teens and young adults because it is always delivered with a preachy pointing swinging finger. I think many are immune to the word and it just deflects, but let me dig a little deeper into its origin. Then you can consider its wise meaning before you order a quadruple cheeseburger with Goliath fries and a Whata-sized Big Gulp followed by a milkshake chaser.

Moderation is not a new concept. It is a principle of life. In ancient Greece an inscription that read Meden Agan could be found in the temple of Apollo at Delphi. It means "nothing in excess" which is another way of saying do stuff "in moderation."

FM, the radio station format most teenagers like to listen to is the abbreviation for Frequency Modulation. The word modulation means exerting a modifying or controlling influence on something. If moderation sounds too stuffy to you, modulation can be used with moderation as a reminder to not eat too many gigantic cheeseburgers or watch too many college basketball games in one sitting. And perhaps you'll continue to appreciate things on a more long-term basis because you didn't wear them out.

Take it easy,
Your papi

 #87 THINGS I WISH I HAD TAUGHT MY SON... AND STILL CAN
Don't get your wires crossed... Part 1.

We're transitioning as a country from standard definition TV to HD (High Definition) TV (these include LCD TVs and Plasma TVs). I'm not sure if you're up to speed with all the names and types of wiring you currently use to get your contraptions to work. So I decided to dedicate this email to 101-ing you on the most common wires and cables and formats you'll need to become familiar with. I'll start with old-school cable still being used. This is the RF cable that usually screws on at two points, at the wall (if you have cable or a satellite feed) or to the back of traditional TVs, VCRs and DVRs. DVRs might have two RF male jacks so that one receiver can record while another plays back. The RF cables are referred to as female. The RF jacks are referred to as male.

The next most common audio and video connectors are called RCA connectors. RCA used to be quite a strong company (Radio Corporation of America). They introduced this technology in the 40s. It was used to connect phono (also called record players, turntables) players to amplifiers. It later became the standard for connecting other Hi-Fi devices. The audio portion of the RCA connectors are usually red and white or red and grey for left and right signals. I believe it must have been the 80s when the yellow connector was added to the red and white duo. The yellow cable is for transferring an analog video signal. To confuse matters even more, there are some similar looking cables at electronic stores that are red, green and blue. They are called component connectors. Some TVs have component "in" jacks. Some DVD players have component "out" jacks. They only transfer video but at a greater color and picture accuracy. If you do use these (they are becoming less common) you still have to use the RCA audio cables to get the audio from a DVD player or VCR to the TV or other form of sound system. Back in the day, S-VHS (Super-VHS) was another promising technology that sharpened the picture a little more to 420 lines of horizontal resolution. A typical VHS (Video Home System) resolution was 240.

I hope you're still tuning in because here comes HD.

Currently at stores, you may have noticed the horizontal widescreeny looking TVs that seem to be everywhere. The old TVs have an aspect ratio of 4:3. Their widescreen counterparts have a 16:9 aspect ratio (aspect ratio = width divided by height). You may think this is not a big deal but wait until you have to make little youtube.com videos for a class. You'll pull your hair out with the many options and aspect ratios that exist.

Back to the wires.

A new handy cable is called HDMI (High Definition Multimedia Interface). It doesn't send analog (sound and video), it sends digital information. All new DVD players, HD-DVD players, Apple TV interfaces and Blu-Ray players connect to these new TVs via HDMI cables. Both images and sound are transferred through this cable. And yep, they are expensive. Why does this HD stuff matter. These new cables send a massive amount of information to these new TVs and these new HD TVs display picture and sound with amazing detail. The picture quality ranges from 720i to 1080p. What used to be 240 or 420 lines of resolutions is now from three to five times (don't hold me to the math) as sharp and vivid. It looks like you're there.

There is a push by the broadcast and cable companies to move old TVs out of circulation next year and you will be forced to learn all this stuff (whether you like it or not). I just thought I would give you a head-start.

And that's just the first set of cables,

> *Disconnecting for now,*
> *Your papi*

 #88 THINGS I WISH I HAD TAUGHT MY SON... AND STILL CAN
Fragile. Open with care...

At about 2 AM this morning, I thought about the fragility of life. I woke up in a panic because your brother was coughing. I thought he was about to throw up so I lifted him up and ran with him to the bathroom. That's when the change of blood flow to my head caught up. That's when I knew that my going from horizontal to vertical in such a mad rush and running with your brother, after my having vomited myself at midnight, would take its toll on me. Since your brother had dibs on the toilet bowl (I thought he was vomiting), I made my way to the sink. I'll spare you the details of that, but I will tell you that I thought I was going to collapse or faint or something. I yelled out for mom with concern but she was in the living room and couldn't hear me.

What I thought of was that I was going to a funeral the next day for two young men. I believe one of the deceased was my age or just slightly older and his kids are younger than you. The other was 22 when a car accident ended his life. I thought about your friend Frankie's father and his recovery from a heart attack. He sat with us, a perfect picture of health, at your graduation breakfast. Perhaps I was being overly dramatic but I was dizzy, weak and consumed with cold chills.

Yesterday was Thanksgiving, and I've been watching hours and hours of video of when you were all younger. I am thankful for the joy your mom and all of you have brought to my life. Had I checked out yesterday, I can joyfully say that I had a full life filled with lots of laughter and happy cries. Don't get me wrong, I'd like to get the extended stay package, but I will continue to live my life fully on a daily basis.

I took a break from this email and stumbled onto a never-before-seen video of Christie on an unlabeled tape. She was at your second oldest sister's seventh birthday party at our house standing behind her (she couldn't resist putting rabbit ears on your sister). Her parents will appreciate this little clip. I include this note because Christie is a wonderful example of someone who seemed to have lived life to the fullest (Christie was washed away in a flash flood two blocks from her house).

The lesson for today: Live life like it is your last day to do so.

> *Thanks for being my son,*
> *Your papi*

 #89 THINGS I WISH I HAD TAUGHT MY SON... AND STILL CAN
Don't get your wires crossed... Part 2.

Because I'm an audio buff and because everybody nowadays needs to know a little about audio cables, here's my 101 on sound. I mentioned that RCA created the phono connectors, the red and white plugs that are used for connecting a wide variety of audio components. Recently there has been a blurring of pro audio with home audio with the advent of computers taking a front stage role in recording and playback.

First off, I'd like to define the mini-plug. The mini-plug is the little headphone-jack size connector that has been used since the first Walkman players were introduced (I know you weren't born yet but these were portable personal cassette and radio players... I feel much older having written this). These little mini-plugs have taken on a new role since most computers have only a mini-sized audio jack for headphones. Originally, they were intended for just headphones but with the advent of MP3s and other formats of music the computer became an entertainment center. That's when the mini-plug became the bridge to the RCA cables. This allowed for the computer to be connected to stereos and amplifiers. Naturally, all CD players and iPods followed suit. People use these mini-plug/

RCA connectors quite a bit. I always carry an extra one in my bag because they are often needed when making presentations.

When headphones came out, they didn't use this mini-plug, they used a 1/4" plug because the width of the plug was 1/4 of an inch. These plug connectors are used for a variety of functions. First of all, they are better than the minis because of their sturdier connection. Secondly, they often connect professional instruments to amplifiers and recording consoles. The 1/4" plugs with one black stripe are mono plugs meaning that only one channel of sound is being transported. The 1/4" plugs with two stripes are stereo plugs. There are many variations that splice this stereo to mono signal but I'll have to show you the differences in person.

The next type of connector is called an XLR. These are robust connectors for professional applications. XLRs are usually the type of connectors used for professional microphones. They have three little male prongs that connect to three little female slots. XLRs are also used to connect Hi-Fi amplified speakers. They also connect to mixing boards. If you're around me, in the line of work I do, you'll come across XLRs frequently.

That's enough techno speak for now.

> *How does that sound?*
> *Your papi*

 #90 THINGS I WISH I HAD TAUGHT MY SON... AND STILL CAN
If a door doesn't open for you...

This morning I went to Home Depot because I was fed up with our laundry room door. It was stuck. No longer could we jiggle it and turn it to open. The knob was a goner. It had to be replaced. I went to Home Depot with a general idea of what to get, but I have to admit, I had never replaced a doorknob before in my life.

When I found the doorknob aisle, of course all the packaging promised "easy installation". Was I in over my head? I got what I needed, went home and got to work. I asked you to help me. Within the first two minutes we were stumped.

When I was a senior in college in Austin, I tried to get an internship at Sosa & Associates. This was an up-and-coming advertising agency in San Antonio. I sent a letter. I got no reply. The metaphorical door wouldn't open. I spoke with the secretary of one of the agency partners. She said they had no internship program. The door wouldn't budge. I spoke to the secretary of the other partner. She said they couldn't accommodate me (I don't remember the reason). That door wasn't going to budge either. I sat in the lobby a few times trying to get a meeting with the president. "Sorry, but Lionel won't be able to meet with you. He's in a meeting and will be leaving shortly thereafter," stated the receptionist. Then I asked for a meeting with Robert Sosa thinking he was the brother of Lionel Sosa. Surely, that was another door I could try to open. Robert quickly told me that he wasn't related to Lionel. He looked at my portfolio and didn't know what to make of it. It was a bit different from what he was used to.

"Listen, I'll work for free. I'm planning on sleeping on my cousin Joelito's living room floor. People won't let me work because I don't have experience, and I can't get experience because nobody will hire me. I can design the internship program myself." I must have sounded pretty desperate because Robert then gets up and walks into Lionel's office. He comes back and says that I'm in and that I will at least get minimum wage. I got the door open. A year later, together with Robert, I won for the agency a Clio Award (the Academy Award equivalent for the advertising industry in those days) followed by 12 more.

I went back to Home Depot asking for a strange tool that hasn't been invented yet. That's because I couldn't remove the screws on account of a faceplate between the knob and the door. The man at the store must have seen how hopeless I looked and sounded so he explained how doorknobs work. He showed me an almost invisible little clip that pops out the knob so that the screws can easily be removed. "Oooooooh! I get it!" I would have never figured it out.

We sort of succeeded. I did the replacement job on one door, you did another. I think we stripped one screw on each of the knobs but hey, we live and learn. At least the doors are now opening and closing easily.

The lesson for today is twofold: The first is that you keep trying to open closed doors if you really want to get ahead because ultimately, it is you who will benefit the people on the other side. The second lesson we did together... It was helping each other learn to change a doorknob. You learned that lesson 25 years sooner than I.

> Go open some doors,
> Your papi

PS: Just as I was about to hit send... I got this wonderful little "Author Unknown" quote from a distant cousin, Luis Ramírez that I met in my genealogical journey.

"LIFE... is not a journey to the grave with the intention of arriving safely in a pretty and well preserved body, but rather to skid in broadside, thoroughly used up, totally worn out, and loudly proclaiming – WOW!!! – WHAT A RIDE!" — *Author Unknown*

✉ #91 THINGS I WISH I HAD TAUGHT MY SON... AND STILL CAN
Become an etymologist...

Regardless of what field of interest you end up choosing as a career, become an amateur etymologist too.

I love words. I love to push them around to see what happens. Sometimes they're feisty. Sometimes they bite. But most of the time you can train them to do tricks. The only way you can do that is if you become an amateur in this fluid world of words. Most people think that amateur means "not good enough to be a pro". The origin of the word is amatory or lover. To be an amateur is to be a lover. Lately, the word as taken on a meaning of ineptness... Not good enough.

If you call me an amateur, I'll say thank you. It means that I do stuff for the love of it. People who do things like painting, coaching or public speaking not for the pay but for the love of it are also amateurs.

Etymology is the study of words. In *Akeelah and the Bee* (a very inspiring movie), the young power speller always learned the origin of a word to help her understand the history behind the word, which in turn helped her remember the words more organically. She knew whether it was originally Greek or Latin or Indo-European. It clued her in on the spelling.

Most good dictionaries have an "origin" entry after they've defined a word. This origin or etymological note will clue you in on where the particular word you are studying has been... And all words have a back story.

Next time you hear an interesting word and you want to consider using it, check the dictionary on your computer or use yourdictionary.com. It has an "ORIGIN" section at the bottom. The word will more likely stick like Velcro in your brain if you know its back story. For example, etymology comes from etymon and logy. First, etymon means the literal sense of a word. Second, logy means science or doctrine or theory. Therefore, if you put those together, you get the study of the literal sense of a word.

> *Don't be afraid to be an amateur,*
> *Your papi*

✉ #92 THINGS I WISH I HAD TAUGHT MY SON... AND STILL CAN
The parable of the cricket...

I can hear my name in a crowded airport. You can hear your ringtone above any other sound in your environment. I can distinguish the serious cries of your baby sister from her fake cries. I tune in when I think I hear something important around me. I tune out when the subject matter doesn't match my interest.

The following is a story that I use in seminars often. It is a short little fable about a cricket.

THE CRICKET!
A Native American and his friend were in downtown New York City, walking near Times Square in Manhattan. It was during the lunch hour and the streets were filled with people. Cars were honking their horns, taxicabs were squealing around corners, sirens were wailing, and the sounds of the city were almost deafening. Suddenly, the Native American said, "I hear a cricket."

His friend said, "What? You must be crazy. You couldn't possibly hear a cricket in all of this noise!"

"No, I'm sure of it," the Native American said, "I heard a cricket."

"That's crazy," said the friend.

The Native American listened carefully for a moment, and then walked across the street to a big cement planter filled with shrubs. He looked into the bushes, beneath the branches, and sure enough, he located a small cricket. His friend was utterly amazed.

"That's incredible," said his friend. "You must have super-human ears!"

"No," said the Native American. "My ears are no different from yours. It all depends on what you're listening for."

"But that can't be!" said the friend. "I could never hear a cricket in this noise."

"Yes, it's true," came the reply. "It depends on what is really important to you. Here, let me show you."

He reached into his pocket, pulled out a few coins, and discreetly dropped them on the sidewalk. And then, with the noise of the crowded street still blaring in their ears, they noticed every head within twenty feet turn and look to see if the money that tinkled on the pavement was theirs.

"See what I mean?" asked the Native American. "It all depends on what's important to you."
— *Author Unknown*

When I finish reading this little story, the audience is now tuned in to what I have to say. I tell this same audience that I will teach them to perceive the crickets that customers from others cultures hear. I then get started.

> *Chirp, chirp,*
> *Your papi*

 #93 THINGS I WISH I HAD TAUGHT MY SON... AND STILL CAN
Don't get your wires crossed... Part 3.

This is the last cable and wire installment. It relates to your computer. I'm not going to assume anything even though you may already be using these cables.

I'll start off with the most universal of cables (at least for now), the USB. Actually, it stands for Universal Serial Bus. In computer-speak, a bus is a subsystem that transfers data between computer components inside a computer or between computers. The USB port on your computer accepts jump drives, iPods, cameras, external hard drives, modems, printers and a whole host of other outside gadgets. Some USB ports put out energy (for recharging devices while others are passive and only transfer data. These little versatile USBs are great and other future technologies will appear as the years go by. There are two main USB cables that you should always have in your computer bag. There is the square type that connects to your printer and to external hard drives and there are the smaller types that connect to digital cameras and other low-powered gadgets. But the USB is also a slow means for transferring large quantities of information.

Enter Firewire. There are two types of Firewire cables (so far)... Firewire 400 and Firewire 800. These can move many gigs (gigabytes) around in minutes. I use a lot of video and a typical video project can run around 30 gigs. I almost exclusively use Firewire 800 cables. The bad news for you is that your computer only has Firewire 400. However, it's good to know about this turbo of cables. In your computer bag you should also always have a regular Firewire cable that is identical on both ends. The other type of Firewire 400 cable is the one used to import video from a digital video camera to your computer.

I've already covered the audio jack that is on your computer. It is a mini jack for headphones and mini plugs that convert to RCA cables.

Finally, Ethernet is the last type of cable that you need to tote in your bag... About 10 feet worth of it. Increasingly, you'll be able to use wireless connections around your campus but once in a while you'll have to go "old school" and plug in. That's it for cables and wires.

> *Don't get tangled up,*
> *Your papi*

 #94 THINGS I WISH I HAD TAUGHT MY SON... AND STILL CAN
The last shall be first... If the line changes directions.

For the next several decades you will have the wonderful opportunity to stand or be in line. Obey the line, stay in line, wait your turn. Society depends on your obedience to this universal concept. When people disobey this important system, everything falls apart. Randomness sets in. People get hurt. Some parents teach their kids to skip the line and try to pretend that there are no people waiting. Not me. The line is a good thing as long as respect for the practice continues to be the order of things.

People who cut or skip or jump the line steal time and life from those who follow the rule. Some people take this to the streets and freeways of our life. They cut people off because they must get to where they're going faster than their adjacent vehicular neighbors. In the process of getting ahead, they bring others to a screeching, even dangerous halt. In the book, *The Wisdom of Crowds*, the author writes about the profound consequences to the flow of traffic resulting from the insensitivity of just a few lane-changers. It affects everybody for miles.

Imagine this... Mr. Insensitive is driving fast down the freeway and spots a tiny opening in the next two lanes. He crosses over and causes the flowing traffic (previously traveling smoothly) on each lane to brake. The car behind each of these cars brakes too because it thinks that something has occurred ahead. The butterfly effect continues for many car lengths. Perhaps a car accident is caused because another lane-changer down the line was not expecting a domino effect ahead of him and gets caught in a mid-lane change. Throw in a couple of 18-wheelers who can't react fast enough and you have a huge traffic mess. Meanwhile, Mr. Insensitive has no clue what he has caused. You shouldn't be that Mr. Insensitive. Not in the cafeteria, not at registration for a new class, not on the road.

While you may miss some opportunities because you end up at the back of a line on some occasions, I guarantee you that in the long run, you will benefit more often from keeping to the norms of the larger society. If you want to be first in line, manage your time better and plan for it.

> *Now get back in line and no cuts,*
> *Your papi*

 #95 THINGS I WISH I HAD TAUGHT MY SON... AND STILL CAN
What are you listening to?

Poetry and musical lyrics have a way of getting past your mind's security system. I was fascinated when I learned this from Roy Williams of The Wizard Academy. He systematically proved his point by playing a few songs, popular songs that we all knew, and then showed us the lyrics to those songs, astonishing us. One was about suicide, the theme song of *M.A.S.H.*, the show. One was about murder, and it was being used in a McDonalds commercial. One was about a bitter Vietnam vet being critical of this country. Meanwhile, Bob Dole was using this song as a theme song for his presidential bid. It turns out that because poetry and music comes in through our right brain, it sneaks in with it thoughts and ideas we would not normally accept were they written down on paper and analyzed by our left brain.

Shaggy's *It Wasn't Me* is an example of a sticky catchy song (check out those lyrics) that made it to the top of the charts while its subject matter was about a guy who denied he was having sex with his neighbor. "It wasn't me" was the main recurring hook in the song. Even though his wife caught him having sex with his neighbor, all he did was deny it... "It wasn't me."

This song was played on regular radio all day long. I'm sure it was played in mini-vans (even ours) filled with kids as mommy sang along. How can this be? How did it get past our censor? Musical catchy lyrics are the kryptonite of our better judgment. One of these days, watch *Hustle & Flow* and witness how easy your brain will cooperate.

I remember discussing the lyrics of Creed's *Six Feet From the Edge* with you after hearing you sing it out loud. At face value it seemed like a straightforward power rock song but the underlying suicide theme can easily be decoded if you see it in print. I won't even comment on a song by Lustra that I recently stumbled upon.

Poetry changes us. One of these days, you will be moved by a passionate poem or carefully syncopated piece of passionate rap. And you'll remember this email.

Never underestimate the power of music and song. Teens and young adults swear they are above being influenced by this music. However, they don't have a fighting chance. These musical hooks are firmly set in their minds just as a fisherman set his hook in the mouth of a game fish. Love songs, hate songs, break-up songs, songs that disrespect women, songs that breed rebellion, they're not powerless.

Fo' shizzle,
Your papi

 #96 THINGS I WISH I HAD TAUGHT MY SON... AND STILL CAN
Pizza love and real love...

Several years ago I stumbled onto a book entitled *Real Love* by Mary Beth Bonacci. The book introduced me to a helpful way to understand and talk about love and sex with teens and young adults. The book introduced me to pizza love.

When a pizza arrives at your door or at your table, you get excited. "Oh I love pizza!", people often say when they start eating away. "I love pizza, too", somebody follows. Everything seems lovey-dovey, gooey and genuine. The second piece and we still say, "I love pizza, yum," and continue enjoying it. The third piece, everything is still delicious. Once we hit the fourth, depending upon the size of our appetite, we begin to get those familiar "I'm stuffed" feelings. During the fifth piece and beyond, words of love about pizza aren't as forthcoming. Sooner or later, we don't care what happens with the leftover pizza. Sometimes, we don't even care if the remainder is thrown in the trash. "Just get it out of my sight."

That my son is pizza love.

I have committed my life to my wife. I did so 20 years ago. I would do anything for her, even give up my life. As the catchy song in the Wedding Singer so eloquently put it, "I want to grow old with you" is the sentiment that drives my thoughts and goals with your mom, my wife. Your mom loves me the same way. She puts me before her. That my son is real love.

I've taught your two oldest sisters the difference between pizza love and real love. I suggested to them that if a boy ever poured out his heart and said, "I love you," they should ask what kind of love he is referring to... Pizza love or real love. Sometimes guys (and increasingly girls) will say "I love you" to get something they want like sex... It sort of speeds things up. The problem with this is that sexual intimacy (a beautiful gift to be shared with somebody you really love), has become as devalued as a sixth piece of pizza. Once the person is so easily used and consumed, they can be thrown away and forgotten. Have you ever heard of a promiscuous person being called trashy?

The responsibility lies with you. All universities have become hooking-up (non-committal sex) centers. Casual sex is more common than good grades it seems. Unfortunately, this type of behavior raises the probability that these young adults will end up in an extremely painful divorce. The most widely quoted stat for the current divorce rate is approximately 50% depending on several life factors. Using the pizza love strategy raises your odds that you'll be on the wrong side of the statistic. I don't want that for you.

I'm not boo-hooing sexual intimacy. I said it is a wonderful gift. Make that gift sacred by accompanying it with a total commitment sealed in real love. Perhaps this is the most uncomfortable email I've sent so far. It's probably utterly uncool and extremely untimely. Still, I send it because I want to have you avoid unimaginable, hard-to-overcome pain, not only for you but also for naive young girls who think that they won't be haunted by their poor judgment for the rest of their lives.

Be counter-cultural. Respect women even though other guys treat them as objects for their personal satisfaction. And pray that some young man out there treats your future wife with the same respect.

> *Trust me on this one,*
> *Your papi*

 #97 THINGS I WISH I HAD TAUGHT MY SON... AND STILL CAN
Harry's song...

When I was around 14 or 15-years-old, I heard a song by Harry Chapin that would haunt me, keep me reflecting about my fatherhood role for my entire life. From the first time I heard it I remembered most of its heart-piercing lyrics. Today I went to a Fatherhood conference at Our Lady of the Lake University. It was a great day of wonderful insight. During a powerful performance from a drama professor at OLLU on the absence of his father, he pulls out the lyrics of this reflective song.

My memory doesn't serve me well but I vaguely remember that I've told you about and played this song, *Cat's in the Cradle*, for you. If I didn't, the following lyrics I am sure have changed the lives of many fathers around the world. The song was a poem written by Harry Chapin's wife. Here it is.

> *A child arrived just the other day,*
> *He came to the world in the usual way.*
> *But there were planes to catch, and bills to pay.*
> *He learned to walk while I was away.*
> *And he was talking 'fore I knew it, and as he grew,*

He'd say, "I'm gonna be like you, dad.
You know I'm gonna be like you."

And the cat's in the cradle and the silver spoon,
Little boy blue and the man in the moon.
"When you coming home, dad?" "I don't know when,
But we'll get together then.
You know we'll have a good time then."

My son turned ten just the other day.
He said, "Thanks for the ball, dad, come on let's play.
Can you teach me to throw?" I said, "Not today,
I got a lot to do." He said, "That's ok."
And he walked away, but his smile never dimmed,
Said, "I'm gonna be like him, yeah.
You know I'm gonna be like him."

And the cat's in the cradle and the silver spoon,
Little boy blue and the man in the moon.
"When you coming home, dad?" "I don't know when,
But we'll get together then.
You know we'll have a good time then."

Well, he came from college just the other day,
So much like a man I just had to say,
"Son, I'm proud of you. Can you sit for a while?"
He shook his head, and he said with a smile,
"What I'd really like, dad, is to borrow the car keys.
See you later. Can I have them please?"

And the cat's in the cradle and the silver spoon,
Little boy blue and the man in the moon.
"When you coming home, son?" "I don't know when,
But we'll get together then, dad.
You know we'll have a good time then."

I've long since retired and my son's moved away.
I called him up just the other day.
I said, "I'd like to see you if you don't mind."
He said, "I'd love to, dad, if I could find the time.

You see, my new job's a hassle, and the kid's got the flu,
But it's sure nice talking to you, dad.
It's been sure nice talking to you."
And as I hung up the phone, it occurred to me,
He'd grown up just like me.
My boy was just like me.

And the cat's in the cradle and the silver spoon,
Little boy blue and the man in the moon.
"When you coming home, son?" "I don't know when,
But we'll get together then, dad.
You know we'll have a good time then."

I guess I should be thankful that this song was always playing in the background of my mind. It's kept me focused on my father role.

I learned a great deal at this conference today. Most of the fathers there did not have a steady father figure and were thirsting for help in this department. I have a wonderful father. I am blessed.

The Fatherhood conference centered me for the next chapters. I sometimes feel like I've reached some imaginary finish line because I have a kid in college, but your two-year-old sister is running around the house with a dirty diaper and expects a lot of attention from me through the milestones of her life. It's just like I'm getting started again.

When you have a kid… I'll send you a copy of Harry's song.

I know you'll have a good time then, son,
Your papi

 #98 THINGS I WISH I HAD TAUGHT MY SON… AND STILL CAN
Start, stop and keep on doing…

About 12 years ago, I learned a helpful technique that can be used to improve friendships, romantic relationships, work environments, business practices, and accountability in clubs and organizations. This three sentence exercise can be used anywhere a person expects some type of positive behavior from the other member or members of a group and vice versa. When consulting, I have used this potent little communication device to work the kinks out of a stagnant team.

The three simple little sentences that had the power to transform the group were the following:

I want you to start _____.

I want you to stop _____.

I want you to keep on _____.

Yes... It's that simple.

About 10 years ago in a little company retreat, the members of the particular meeting were all filling in the blanks. I was the recipient of their suggestions. I was the one who would be doing the starting, stopping and keeping on. I distinctly remember somebody from the office stating that I buried myself in my work and my computer and I should start walking around, getting to know the people who work with or for me. Another person said I had a built-in "you-look-like-you're-angry" frown on my face. They suggested I stop looking so intense and smile more often. In the keep on doing department, a suggestion came up that I keep on teaching the newbies at our office the particular brand of marketing that I believed in. Everybody in the group of six or seven all gave me a start, stop and keep on doing suggestion. I had plenty of feedback to work with.

This type of forum allows for constructive criticism and it often yields some easy-to-implement suggestions. Perhaps, one day you may find yourself in a leadership role needing a method for giving acknowledgement, inspiration and constructive correction. You may find yourself trying to improve a sports team where the same mistakes keep recurring and where talent is not being exploited correctly. You may just be talking with your girlfriend and want to find a way to improve your communication and expectations.

Just start, stop and keep on doing.

> *Keep on making me proud,*
> *Your papi*

 #99 THINGS I WISH I HAD TAUGHT MY SON... AND STILL CAN
You're going to need it... In the futuro.

According to the writers of *The Story of English* there were about a million words in the English language in 1992... 500,000 from the *Oxford English Dictionary* and another half-million technical and scientific terms. Of course, that was before the Internet and before the heyday of rap and hip hop. We've got many more bling bling and iPoddy terms now. These are currently the most popular words in the English language... the, be, to, of, and, a, in, that, have, I, it.

I took a five minute quiz at the following website: http://quizicon.com/100-Most-Common-English-Words-Quiz.html. I wanted to see how many of the top 100 words I could guess. I didn't do very well. Most of these top 100 words are navigation words, articles, short adjectives and pronouns. Most of them have their origin in Old English.

I recently watched *My Big Fat Greek Wedding*. In the movie, the proud papa constantly reminded his daughter and anybody else who would listen that many words come from the Greek language. One estimate that I read in a book about the history of Latin was that 35% of the English language has Greek origins. It continued that 50% of all English words are Latin derivatives. The remainder comes from Old English and a smattering of other languages.

Today's lesson is that you take an interest in the first language you learned to speak as a baby, Spanish. Perhaps it will take a beautiful girl or a business opportunity to get you on the fast-track to relearning your mother tongue. The future will most certainly demand that you become a polyglot. Considering the interest you take in Biology, you may be learning full-speed ahead already since many terms like phylum (from phulon), class (from the clasis), genus, and species (from specere) are Latin. I sort of feel like the Greek Wedding dad now.

Learning Spanish and even cooler, Latin, will give you a leg up in this inter-lingual world. Albanian, Spanish, Portuguese, Catalan, French, Italian, and Romanian all share different amounts of the Latin lexicon. They are called the Romance languages. I want you to be connected to your ancient heritage. Your second oldest sister has taken an interest in Japanese and French and she has also test-driven Latin. Why not brush up on what will naturally return once you put out a welcome mat.

Spanish has much to offer you. About 350 million people speak Spanish around the world. Knowing it will open puertas.

> *Now get back to clase,*
> *Tu papi*

PS: Tomorrow will be a milestone for me. I'm having a wonderful time doing this for you and your younger brothers and sisters. Hasta manana.

#100 THINGS I WISH I HAD TAUGHT MY SON... AND STILL CAN
Don't be late...

A library book is free to check out if you return it within the alloted time. Otherwise, the free becomes a fee. Red Box (the cheap video rental box outside McDonalds) is $1 if you get it back by 9 PM the next day.

Entire industries are counting on your and my being late to return rented stuff to make their year-end profits. Ruin their day. Get stuff back on time. Let somebody else make a contribution to their bottom line, not you. Exorbitant late fees are the most insidious practices of credit card companies and car rental companies, to mention a few of the usual suspects (Blockbuster Video's "end of late fees" advertising campaign is also a sham).

These fees are absolutely avoidable. Heck, late fees can sometimes be more costly than the purchase price of some of the items you rent. That's just wrong! Late fee repeat offenders are the preferred type of customers of many companies. They reward these forgetful renters with incentives to be late again. I'm surprised they don't get a t-shirt in the mail.

The companies that assess late fees do so by the day (but it seems it's by the hour). They just charge and charge and charge while you look under the couch for pennies to complete your lunch money. They gouge while you wear dirty jeans because you didn't have enough for the laundromat.

Sharing late fee one-upmanship stories with your friends will not make these wrongs right. It's an utter waste of money to be charged these fees and you should squash them.

Lately, I've been reviewing your recent late fees. Actually, your mom brought it to my attention. I can't throw the first stone because I've been guilty of this expensive oversight myself, but I can tell you that the sophistication and accompanying repercussions from late fee-loving companies are much greater. These pesky fees add up. Left unattended, they may add up to a car or house payment. Don't let that happen.

> *It's late. I'm going to sleep,*
> *Your papi*

 #101 THINGS I WISH I HAD TAUGHT MY SON... AND STILL CAN
Super Foods... An acquired taste... And acquired health too...

Earlier this year, I read a book (actually I listened to the audio book) about the most powerful, most nutritious foods on the planet. These foods, according to authors Dr. Steven Pratt and

Kathy Matthews, have the power to change your biochemistry. All these yummy comestibles are all credited with preventing and sometimes reversing heart disease, diabetes, some cancers and dementia.

Here they are...

Beans (all kinds)... Four 1/2 cup servings per week
Blueberries (raspberries and cranberries too)... Eat two cups daily
Broccoli... 1/2 to 1 cup daily
Oats... Five to seven servings a day
Oranges... One serving daily
Pumpkin... 1/2 cup daily
Wild salmon... Two to four times a week
Soy (not the Spanish word for I am)... 15 grams a day
Spinach (not the cartoon type)... One cup steamed or two cups raw daily
Green tea... One or more cups daily
Tomatoes... One serving per day
Turkey... Four 4-ounce servings per week
Walnuts and almonds (raw)... One ounce, five times a week
Yogurt... Two cups daily

Take notice that popcorn and nachos are not on the *Super Foods* list. I don't think pizza will be knocking beans or broccoli from the top spots.

During Thanksgiving you mentioned that you gained the freshman 15 (the associated weight gain that comes with being a fish) from the abundant carb rich food on your meal plans. You're quite thin so this weight gain wasn't a big deal but your metabolism will slow as you get older if the above-mentioned food (or foods like them) do not become part of your diet. I'm sure that some of these foods are available at your cafeteria if you look around carefully. Perhaps you don't have an appetite for some of these now but learning to like them and then to love them will serve you well. At your age, you can indefinitely detour many of the diseases that may show up when you're in your late 30s and early 40s.

I feel a cliché coming now as I close this email. It is "you are what you eat."

Does that mean I'm a turkey? A nut?

> *Yo soy what I eat,*
> *Your papi*

✉ #102 THINGS I WISH I HAD TAUGHT MY SON... AND STILL CAN
I love nopal... Without thorns, of course.

I've been paying attention to this soon-to-be Super Food. I drink it in juice form. I mix the dehydrated form in juices too (although I'm not crazy about its powdery texture). I eat it for breakfast, lunch and dinner at one of the taquerias, usually with a delicious cut of meat called abujas.

Nopal is cactus... Opuntia Cactaceae in scientific terms.

I used to go to a juice bar and the owners would specially make a nopal/carrot juice blend or a nopal/orange juice blend. They thought I was a bit weird. Then I went to Monterrey on a business trip and found the same concoction on the menu at a diner.

When I was your age, I went to Nuevo Laredo to eat some scrumptious flautas. La Unica was the name of the place. One of the girls that had gone with us was blabbing off a litany of positive attributes about nopal. She ordered a pile of them. She mentioned that the Japanese were exporting all they could get of this prickly phenomena. This was 1984. I listened but thought she was a little loopy.

About ten years ago, I started flirting with this tangy green-beany tasting miracle food that was used by the Aztecs as a staple for centuries. I have it alone or mixed with eggs and shredded jerky. Yummy! Medicinally, this plant (called a vegetable by the USDA) is used by curanderos and holistic food connoisseurs. Its stems and flowers have been used to treat diabetes, stomach problems, fatigue, shortness of breath, easy bruising, prostate enlargement and liver disease. It is a significant source of protein, vitamins and minerals. The latter is true, the former is being backed up with current research findings that I have yet to get my hands on.

All indicators suggest that the loopy girl was right: nopal rocks. I contacted an exporter of a nopal juice extract and he promised to send me a new European study supporting the past claims made by this prickly wonder food.

One of these days, I believe nopal will be right up there in the *Super Foods* hall of fame. If you can, work on acquiring a taste for this up-and-coming health food. That's the hand-me-down lesson for today...

> I'm just trying to Opuntia in a healthy direction (that was a bad pun but I'll keep it),
> Your papi

#103 THINGS I WISH I HAD TAUGHT MY SON... AND STILL CAN
"I may not be there yet, but I'm closer than I was yesterday..." – *Author Unknown*

I embarked on a journey with you more than a 100 days ago. I've been writing this life lesson, found wisdom, how-to email series and doing my homework just as much as you. I got the idea to do this a few days before your freshman college year began and just started. I didn't look back or think about how it would be a burden. I didn't dwell on how it would probably be un-doable. I just jumped in.

This project is transforming me. In fact, I needed it. Thank you.

Today's lesson is about persistence. This is the keep on keeping-on email. Persistence is a very important mental and spiritual muscle that you would be wise to develop. This stick-to-it-ness ability can get you to the hope destinations you have designated that you'd like to arrive at.

This email would be much less credible if this was email #3, and not #103, but we've traveled together past the 100 milestone. I'm going to persist and continue on this trek. This coincides with the last week of your first semester in college. Congratulations as you make it down the last stretch of this first step. Many young college students drop out before the end of their first semester. You persisted.

> *Hold your head up high,*
> *Your papi*

 #104 THINGS I WISH I HAD TAUGHT MY SON... AND STILL CAN
How to .com or .org or website...

Websites are the storefronts of the future. They are the lobbies of clubs and organizations. They are the megaphones of a political campaign. They are genealogical museums, art galleries, poetry anthologies, digital meeting rooms.

In a college context, a website can become your part-time job that works while you do something else. Any club or organization that you join may need a Webmaster for a temporary project. Social network sites like Facebook.com are very powerful but you may often have a need for a site where you need to have total control.

During the holidays I'm going to show you how to make a website from scratch. The entire process will take about 30 minutes, maybe less. I will explain the way hosting services like godaddy.com work including how domain names are found and registered. I will explain how a Web 2.0 site works and how it is superior to the previous sites built several years ago.

Having the ability to make websites for you and for others is akin to knowing how to cook or knowing a little about carpentry. Millions of people still have a need for those who know how to build a website because they have something to sell. Making websites for people is like having a job with flexible hours. Making websites is still a construction-type job but Instead of using hammers and drills, you use files and web skills.

I just recently completed funeralplanningchecklist.org. I mentioned earlier in email #35 (about word tracking) that I would be selling a book for Marnie McDonald, a writer who spent many months researching and putting together a very complete funeral and estate planning guide. This PDF book is designed to help people save time, money and to help restore peace of mind by eliminating the guesswork that accompanies the funeral event. I found her because I bought her book. I think it is a great value. I offered to partner with her to help gain a larger audience for her powerful book.

See you in a few days.

> *Be confident in your final exams,*
> *Your papi*

 #105 THINGS I WISH I HAD TAUGHT MY SON... AND STILL CAN
What Margaret said...

I didn't go to school with Margaret Young. I never had a conversation with her, nor have I ever listened to one of her recordings (I think). During her short recording career, Margaret forever left her child-like, girlish but appealing vocals for the world to enjoy. Among some of those songs were favorites like *Oh! By Jingo! Oh! By Gee!, Stingo Stungo, Jimbo Jambo* and *Oogie Oogie Wa-Wa* (kind of sounds like some hip-hop song lyrics).

I didn't know her because she was born on February 23, 1891. She was a singer and comedienne in the 1920s. She was a Vaudeville singer.

So what do Margaret and I have in common? She said something, a quote that I stumbled onto last night. I don't know the context in which she said it. All I know is that she wants me to write about it today. Funny how wisdom has a way of surviving.

This is what she said:

"Often people attempt to live their lives backwards; they try to have more things, or more money, in order to do more of what they want, so they will be happier. The way it actually works is the reverse. You must first be who you really are, then do what you need to do, in order to have what you want."

People often postpone "living". They want to get the job, the house, the kids, the 401K, the manicured lawn, the latest car... The trappings of a happy life. But they didn't stumble onto Margaret Young's wisdom soon enough. Sometimes, these planaholics, workaholics, and successaholics so intent on getting to their "happy" destination forget to look out the window of life as they zoom by their youth.

There is a "dicho", a proverb, I have heard over the last 10 years by many recent immigrants from Mexico: "Allá en Mexico, se trabaja para vivir. Aquí en los estados unidos, se vive para trabajar." Here is the English rendition of that: "Back in Mexico, people work to live. Here in the United States, people live to work."

Today's lesson is simple. Backwards don't live (I flopped the words for effect). Be who you really are. Be happy in order to get what you want. And as one of Margaret's songs recorded on November 1924 suggests, be *A New Kind of Man*.

> Margaret will stay young forever,
> Your papi

 ### #106 THINGS I WISH I HAD TAUGHT MY SON... AND STILL CAN
I've got Questians...

For the last four years, I have subscribed to Questia. I don't know why I haven't let you and the rest of my kids know about it. Since those days when you were looking for backup for the middle school science fair projects to research papers in high school, you could have benefited from this subscription that I have.

Why?

Questia has 70,000 books and two million articles that are complete and searchable by topic, by word and can be searched by recency. I was preparing to write an email to you about oxytocin when I remembered that I had this valuable resource at my fingertips. The oxytocin article is coming but I thought I would send you my user name and password for Questia. This is perfect for writing a paper because you don't have to go to the library at all and it is open 24/7 unlike libraries. With that many books, articles and journal articles, you'll be sure to find something on whatever you have to write your paper on. In the event that you do need to access a journal article that isn't in the Questia database, it will tell you exactly which libraries have it and how far the library is from you.

http://www.questia.com/tellafriend/?qfe=jramirez467

One of the really helpful tools on the website keeps track of all the books you make a footnote or citation from and then when you're done with the paper, you just click a button and it generates the entire bibliography in one of five popular styles so you can just print it out. When I was teaching at the University of Austin at San Antonio, I used it extensively and I believe I will dust it off again and start using it more often.

> *If you have any questians on Questia text me or give me a call,*
> *Your papi*

 #107 THINGS I WISH I HAD TAUGHT MY SON... AND STILL CAN
The search is on...

I can find almost anything (Internet-wise) I'm looking for on Google... And quick. I guess I assumed that you already knew this lesson, but now I realize that there are millions who don't know these little power tricks. I remember the feeling of power when I learned that if I put "quotes" around a phrase, I could find those exact words on the Internet.

To explain the examples below more clearly I'm going to use brackets [ ] to explain stuff. Don't put brackets [ ] in your Google search, though. I'm just using them to isolate the words in order to better explain this stuff.

Here we go...

If you want to find an exact phrase on Google, this is what you do. You put the exact phrase inside quotes like this:

["two roads diverged in a yellow wood"]

If you type these words into the Google search blank you will find websites all around the world that have used this specific word combination (and in the same sequential order). Most probably, the first entry you will find is Robert Frost's poem, *The Road Not Taken*. After that you'll find every other incidence of "two roads diverged in a yellow path" listed under it. Actually, I tried it myself and did find Robert Frost's *The Road Not Taken* as the first listing. That's what I expected. However, it seems that a man named James Ostrowski also wrote a book entitled *Two Roads Diverged in a Yellow Wood* (not what I was looking for).

Keep in mind that if a professor believes that a student has plagiarized a piece of work, all he or she has to do is take a couple of random sentences from a submitted essay and find it on the Internet. That student will be busted… Bad consequences.

If you type [two diverged path yellow in a roads] (I jumbled up the order) without quotes, you will get all sites in the world that have these words. However, if you are looking for Robert Frost's poem, it may not show up until several pages later. It all depends on the popularity of the phrase. Google's predictive modeling is being improved all the time.

If you want to find one or more of a specific set of words (perhaps because you don't know the exact phrase), you can type [OR] between the words you are including in your search. The following [Road OR Path OR Diverged OR Forest] should result in sites with those words in it.

I once found our genealogy dating back to the 1600s because I put the name Ramirez and Guerrero and Viejo and Tamaulipas in the Google search blank in quotes. ["Ramirez Guerrero Viejo Tamaulipas"]

If you put a minus sign before a word in your search query, [- word] you'll instruct Google to not show you any sites with that unwanted word.

If you're looking for a picture, you can click the [Images] hyperlink at the top of your screen, right under the url. This will only show you sites with pictures that match your search. All you will see are pictures.

If you go to google.com, there are several other powerful options you can select and sort with if you click the "Advanced" hyperlink. They are:

Date (how recent the page is), Usage Rights (this lets you know if something is free to use or licensed), Location of Keywords (where on the page your search can be found… the header, the title, on links, etc), Region (the country in which the sites are located) and Numeric Range (this could be a number range or dollar value).

If you forget this and need to review this again, just click the Advanced button at Google. com. Otherwise search more powerfully.

> *Now if I can only find my keys,*
> *Your papi*

✉ **#108 THINGS I WISH I HAD TAUGHT MY SON... AND STILL CAN**
✉ **You were up to your neck in alligators...**

We were at Sea World, just you and I. Mom trusted me with you and we went for a little excursion. I don't know how old you were, perhaps 3 or 4, but I do remember that you loved dinosaurs and their cousins the alligators. And that's what you wanted to do... Go watch the alligators.

We finally found them. They were sort of close-by the man-made beach area. They were surrounded by a retaining wall and passers-by watched them from behind some post fences (I think they were cedar). We looked on. You looked on in awe and excitement. To get a better view, you tried to position your head between the two horizontal poles. I wasn't paying close attention and I hadn't noticed that your head had become lodged between two poles.

We looked on for a bit more and then it was time to go. But you couldn't get your head out.

I tried to remain calm (but I wasn't), but hey, your head was stuck between two poles! I was on my knees lower than you trying to free you. I tried to turn your little head (actually it was a little big) and coach you to slip back and down. You couldn't understand and probably sensed my concern. By this time both of us had attracted some attention.

"Rafa... Voltea tu cabeza, voltea tu cabeza," is what I said because you mostly understood Spanish in those early years. "Turn you head, turn your head."

Finally, another young man, probably a few years older than me, came to our rescue. He approached us, "Can I help?" I agreed. He freed you.

What did he do?

I was trying to turn your head and coach you back down through the poles and it wasn't working. He instead pulled you up through the poles. He just reached in and grabbed you from your armpits and lifted you. Your head was bigger than your body so your little torso and legs slipped easily through. I felt so stupid. Why didn't I see that?

The lesson for today is perspective. Sometimes, we may be smart and have lots of great ideas, but we don't have a good perspective on a specific situation or on a specific problem. The man who picked you up saw the solution from his angle. I couldn't see it.

I have been selling my perspective on specific marketplace problems for 20 years. It has made many companies millions of dollars, some hundreds of millions.

Still, I have sought the perspective of friends and sages set along my journey to help me see flaws in myself from time to time... And that's worth more than millions.

That's how I see it,
Your papi

 #109 THINGS I WISH I HAD TAUGHT MY SON... AND STILL CAN
What are the odds?

We were excited expectant parents and we knew things were fragile because we had already experienced two miscarriages. To prepare for your arrival, your mom and I went to several Lamaze classes (five or maybe six of them). In the calmness of a meeting room, we sat on a floor with several other pregnant couples. Our nurse coach prepared us for what to expect, what to do, what signs to look for, and how to breath.

Soon you were kicking to get out and Dr. Treviño said it was time for you to arrive. We ran back home, grabbed a few things and soon enough your mom was admitted and wired up for the delivery. We monitored your every heartbeat, the distance between contractions, etc...

You took your time. And mami was in pain. Every time the contractions arrived, your mom was very uncomfortable. All the while I was trying to remember what I had learned in Lamaze. I'll tell you later about Dr. Lamaze in another email.

Anyway, your mom thought she would share the pain a little and decided that it would be okay if she dug her fingernails into the back of my hand every time you created a contracting ruckus. I know this is not a fair comparison to the actual pain that accompanies the delivery of a baby, but still, I wondered if she would tear off a chunk of my hand. Meanwhile, I had to remember hee hee hoo, hee hee hoo (the breathing exercises we had gone over many times), which I'm sure, annoyed her a bit too. I think we arrived at the hospital at about 5 PM on the seventh of March but you wouldn't arrive until the 8th at 12:08 AM.

The odds that you were born are incredibly small. The odds that your mom and I, who were born 1,400 miles away from each other, would meet, fall in love and make a life together and then have you is a number with enough zeroes on the right side of a decimal point to make you dizzy.

So... relatively speaking, the odds of your being successful and doing wonderful things with your life are quite large in comparison.

> *You'll do great things... I'm betting on it,*
> *Your papi*

 #110 THINGS I WISH I HAD TAUGHT MY SON... AND STILL CAN
Hang with me...

I have a stud finder. That's what you call the contraption that finds the hidden two inch by four inch (more commonly called 2 x 4s) pieces of wood that are usually used in the construction of a typical room's frame. Studs are almost always invisible to the eye. That's because they are usually covered with sheet rock panels, taped at the seams and then smoothed out. Done right, you can't tell that there are several panels of sheet rock covering the walls... It just looks like one continuous piece.

Earlier today, your next youngest brother was decorating the room he shares with his two youngest brothers. I heard him hammering away and it piqued my curiosity. "What is he hammering?" I got up and found him driving nails into sheet rock walls. He was hanging some pictures. I figured it was time for a lesson.

I went and got the stud finder and tape measure. I then returned to his room. Although I am no Bob Villa, I thought it would be a good idea to explain to him and a visiting friend that right above the light switch, where your brother was nailing, were live electrical wires. I mentioned to him that these electrical wires usually run straight up into the attic or down to the floor. He didn't know this. Guess what... When I was his age, I didn't know either. "Did you know this?"

I also explained to the boys that there are studs behind the wall. I used the stud finder to show them where they were located along the wall. I explained that the customary distance between one stud and another (in the United States) is 16 inches from center to center. I explained that very light things like pictures and posters can easily be hung with thumb tacks. However, I mentioned that if they plan to hang some shelves or a flat screen TV (which often weights quite a bit) that they should find the hidden studs and secure their screws or nails to these stable pieces of the construction.

> *File this away on your mental shelf,*
> *Your papi*

✉ **#111 THINGS I WISH I HAD TAUGHT MY SON... AND STILL CAN**
Constructive cataclysmic criticism...

I used to hate getting critiqued. I used to hate the opinions of others as they took shots at my ideas. I couldn't pay attention to the advice being given because I couldn't separate my self from my work. As you know, I have a career that calls for coming up with ideas... For commercials, inventions, marketing campaigns, songs, etc... In order to find some of these ideas floating in my mind's ocean, I have to get personal... With myself. I have to deep dive into past memories and look for idea treasures. I try to see if I can come back up to the surface with an experience that'll work to solve the problem at hand.

Because coming up with an idea is so personal, it can become difficult to take criticism for that newborn baby of an idea. Whether the comments are coming from a well-wisher or from an experienced idea-molder, it can seem that it physically hurts to get anything less than raving applause. I used to think that if an idea (that I came up with) was being chopped up and criticized, then I too was being chopped up and criticized. I had a real fear that made me even more fearful of creating another idea. It was a horrible vicious cycle of gut wrenching.

Once I learned to see an idea as just that, an idea and not a piece of me, then I could free my emotions from having a freak-out party. Now I can actually hear and process the words and feedback given. Sometimes the feedback is, in my estimation, completely unfounded and bogus. Sometimes the insight is bulls-eye on target, uplifting, empowering. This type of feedback may sometimes improve my idea or may prompt me to chunk it in the trash and come up with another.

Before, I used to think that I had only a finite amount of ideas and would one day run out. Now I feel like I will run out of time and energy to write, produce or develop all the ideas that keep coming.

The lesson for today is that you learn to embrace constructive criticism unemotionally by disconnecting yourself from the idea for the brief period in which the idea is being critiqued. Once you have listened intently, then you can re-connect with your idea and take it to the next level of improvement. After all, there are lots more where that one came from.

>   *Get the idea,*
>   *Your papi*

✉ #112 THINGS I WISH I HAD TAUGHT MY SON... AND STILL CAN
The line I want you to avoid...

On the morning of March 3rd 1945, a young man marched into a hilly town named Bitburg, Germany. This man was almost exactly the age that you are now, 15 days before his 19th birthday. The German soldiers were retreating and this young soldier's task was to check that straggler German soldiers were not hiding in buildings. He and a fellow soldier carefully entered a barn that was somehow built into a hillside. Below him was a creek or river. He went down the stairs into the farmhouse. His partner was behind him. A few hundred yards away in the edge of a thicket an 88 millimeter anti-tank gun took aim. Inside that gun, a 30-pound, 36-inch round awaited its mission.

Two days ago, I held in my hand a piece of iron shaped like the Prudential (piece of the rock) logo. I had held it before when I was your age. This little piece of iron almost kept you and I from coming into existence. This four or five ounce piece of iron was part of a 20 pound projectile that sped through the late morning of March 3rd on its way to the barn. On impact the projectile exploded sending shrapnel in all directions. The other soldier who had not yet descended the stairs was killed instantly by the massive explosion. Since he was already going downstairs, the other young man caught the fragments of ricochet. Some hit him in the chin. Another large piece impacted him in the thigh. That's the piece I was holding in my hand a couple of days ago. That 18-year-old man who caught the ricochet of "The 88" is your grandfather, my father. He was sent by the United States to be in the line of fire for the rest of us. He survived. He was blessed to continue on his journey. Even though he flat-lined (died) and almost had his leg amputated, he came back to finish a few more chapters of his story.

The lesson for today: Don't put yourself in the line of fire. Gun deaths, car accident deaths, mistaken identity deaths, careless deaths, unsafe condition deaths, they are all on the rise. Be keenly aware of your surroundings. Find patterns of inconsistencies in people's behavior. Have your intuition listen for sounds of machines that are about to malfunction. Feel for bumps along the road that are different from the previous bumps. Instruct your taste to warn you when a food is not healthy. Smell out smoke, toxic chemicals, danger.

No... I don't want you to be paranoid. I just want you to avoid... Unsafe, unpleasant, unhealthy situations.

> *Or that would be uncool,*
> *Your papi*

PS: A few weeks ago I mentioned that I went to a small class reunion from the class of '83. Yesterday afternoon, one of those classmates, Roland Gonzalez, entered his eternal life. What I know of his untimely death is that an explosion (he worked around highly pressurized wells) caught him off guard. The last conversation I had with him revolved around his demanding work and our quest for finding comfortable shoes. We had a few laughs. We shared a meal. We said goodbye. He too was reading along with these "things" I send you. One of the last emails (#33) he read was the one I wrote about my mother… On celebrating life… Even in death.

I'm going to pray for him and his family… And I'm going to celebrate his life. Pray for them too.

 #113 THINGS I WISH I HAD TAUGHT MY SON… AND STILL CAN
You're their superhero…

Your five-year-old brother thinks the moon is in the sky because you hung it up there. When he grows up he wants to dribble a basketball like you (he was slapping it around). He made this statement a few minutes ago before he went to sleep.

Earlier tonight he was singing *Bless Every Beast* (a Christmas song he sang at his Christmas pageant) when you passed by. You passed by again and told him you heard him singing. Excited that his hero had heard him singing (this is his singing debut) he asked if you liked it. You thought it would be funny to say "no". Ouch!

Had you looked a little closer, you would have seen that he was wearing a shirt with the words, "I'm the little brother." That would make you the big brother. And big brothers have a big job. They inspire. They leave deep tracks in the journey of life so that the little brothers can find their way. Wherever you go, they will eagerly follow. Since you've been back for the holidays, your three younger brothers have been clinging to you for love and attention. They've even risked a little roughhousing pain to get in your good graces.

You are a great big brother 99.99% of the time. Any little brother would be ecstatic to have you as his hero. Last night was just one of those .01% moments that can still be corrected with some words of encouragement. I'm not writing these words without looking squarely into my life mirror. In my role as a father, I have needed to go back to do some patch-up work where I have inflicted unintentional self-esteem cracks.

At this juncture, you may have a more important role than I in molding the activities and dreams your little brothers pursue… That's a cool responsibility. All your sisters love you and admire you too. They know you care for them, their safety, their life decisions. Be conscious of your big brother role as it relates to them too.

"There is no other love like the love for a brother. There is no other love like the love from a brother." — *Astrid Alauda*

Your papi

 #114 THINGS I WISH I HAD TAUGHT MY SON... AND STILL CAN
A giant mutant gift of love...

The following is a little email story I received when you were eight-years-old. I have kept it in my computer all these years and I thought of it today when I saw the gesture your brother did as we opened gifts. Read this:

A FULL BOX OF KISSES
The story goes that some time ago, a man punished his three-year-old daughter for wasting a roll of gold wrapping paper. Money was tight and he became infuriated when the child tried to decorate a box to put under the Christmas tree.

Nevertheless, the little girl brought the gift to her father the next morning and said, "This is for you, Daddy." He was embarrassed by his earlier overreaction, but his anger flared again when he found the box was empty. He yelled at her, "Don't you know that when you give someone a present, there's supposed to be something inside it?"

The little girl looked up at him with tears in her eyes and said, "Oh, Daddy, it is not empty. I blew kisses into the box. All for you, Daddy."

The father was crushed. He put his arms around his little girl, and he begged for her forgiveness. It is told that the man kept that gold box by his bed for years and whenever he was discouraged, he would take out an imaginary kiss and remember the love of the child who had put it there.

Your mom once received a gift-wrapped box with two old pennies, a paper clip, a comb and a used eraser (back in the day we used those for pencils with worn erasers) from your Aunt Patti. Your mom cried when she got the gift. It was a gift of love. The gift cost 2¢ but the estimated price of the love transferred in that little box was priceless (No... This is not a MasterCard commercial).

Your youngest brother parted with his Godzilla toy this Christmas. He thought about you and what you would like. A replica of a fire-breathing radioactive mutant giant dragon is what he thought you would like (remember you're his superhero). I loved your reaction to his "gift of love." He was mildly embarrassed but completely proud.

I expect you to take that Godzilla doll with movable extremities, head and tail to college with you and place it on a shelf of reverence. I'm sure you already thought of that, though.

Perhaps next semester, if we go up to visit you in your dorm, maybe your little brother will tag along and we'll see the gleam in his proud eyes when he sees Godzilla guarding your dorm room from un-welcomed intruders.

Grrrrrrrr,
Your papi

 #115 THINGS I WISH I HAD TAUGHT MY SON... AND STILL CAN
God was painting again...

I don't remember how old I was when I started noticing them myself but there was a beautiful sunset during our drive last night. Did you notice it? We were in different cars and you were 20 minutes ahead of me so I didn't point it out.

I collect sunset experiences. I think I started putting them in my mind's scrapbook when I got married. When it rains in the hill country at about 3 or 4 PM, you can expect a glorious sunset. The water on the ground bounces the light back into the sky in an array of subtle splashes of hues ranging from deep blue to pink to hot bright orange-yellow.

You don't have to go far to find breathtaking sunsets (or sunrises if you wake early enough), but you do have to a find yourself on a good vantage point (a freeway overpass, a hilly part of town, a tall building, a mountaintop, an open highway, etc). Your mom and I have collected a few wonderful sunsets and sunrises in our travels. When I converted my frequent flyer points and went to Hawaii with your mother, we set the camera on a tripod (with the timer) and photographed ourselves with a gigantic sunset behind us. To make it extra special the sunset was over the ocean creating a sparkling effect.

During that same trip, we drove up Mt. Haleakala (a dormant volcano in Maui) in the darkness and waited in almost freezing temperatures to watch the sun rise over the crater of the volcano. I also remember my mom was getting an angioplasty (a procedure that helps dilate blocked arteries) in an early Corpus Christi morning. The waiting room of the hospital overlooks the Gulf of Mexico. On that morning glittering streaks of light cut through the water as the dome of the sun rose above the water.

There are hundreds more that I can mention but describing them will never do them justice.

You will have to soak up your own sunsets. The lesson for today: Stop what you're doing when you see a magnificent sunset arriving. Just watch it. God is painting.

Now you're set,
Your papi

 #116 THINGS I WISH I HAD TAUGHT MY SON… AND STILL CAN
The tools of the trade… Part 1.

Perhaps you have to tighten, loosen, remove, or assemble something. Maybe you need to replace a handle or some other broken part of a machine or appliance. What are you going to use?

SCREWDRIVERS

Henry F. Phillips was a businessman from Portland, Oregon who has the honor of having the crosshead (it's like a plus sign) screw and screwdriver named after him. Before his persuasive attempt to convince screwmakers and automobile companies to adopt this new design, the prevailing type of screw was the slot (this one looks like a minus sign) screw. Some furniture still uses the slot (minus-looking) screw in their construction. Today, the most common screw and screwdrivers are the Phillips type. Another type of tool that is quite common is the Allen or Hex key that is used on hex screws. This tool looks like an L and comes in different sizes. It usually has six sides and fits snugly into the hex screw head… Allowing you to tighten or loosen the screw. Quite often they come included with an item that needs to be assembled.

Some new-fangled computers and machines use Torx, Polydrive, Spine Drive and Double Hex designs for the head. You can see these at the following website. http://en.wikipedia.org/wiki/Hex_key.

THE WRENCH

Wrenches including socket wrenches, crescent wrenches, (also called ratchets) and pipe wrenches are also common tools used in and around cars. The wrench has been around since the 1830s. The most common is the open-ended wrench and the box-end wrench. The open-ended wrench looks like the letter "C" facing up. Box-end wrenches look like a complete circle at each of the ends. These, as well as socket wrenches, come in fractional sizes or in metric sizes (the most common sizes are 7/16 inch, 1/2 inch, and 9/16). Using the wrong size of wrench (or using a metric wrench when a fractional wrench is needed) will cause the destruction of the bolt head or nut making it next to impossible to remove or tighten. How will you know? If you have wiggle room when you attempt to tighten a bolt or nut, you are probably about to ruin either or both.

Socket wrenches or ratchets allow you to work faster and in hard to reach places. You can add extenders to ratchets so that the socket wrench reaches all the way into the tight spots. There are shallow sockets and deep sockets… Specialized by the type of job they are best suited for.

Most of the wrenches are for automobile (bike, motorcycle, etc) work although pipes and faucets also call for this tool. The crescent wrench is adjustable in size and versatile although if used improperly, it can ruin bolts and nuts. For plumbing, the Stinson or pipe wrench is used to loosen and tighten pipes. You can see a pipe wrench here… http://en.wikipedia.org/wiki/Pipe_wrench.

There are more tools to come. You will undoubtedly need them going forward. When you get in a bind.

The last wrench that I want to mention is the lug wrench to remove the five lug nuts that hold a tire in place. This has traditionally been designed in the shape of a cross but in a quest to save money, car companies have included a cheap (often useless) obtuse-angle L shaped wrench. Today, lug nuts are removed at tire shops with pneumatic impact wrenches. However, when stranded in the middle of nowhere, you'll need the lug wrench.

This is just a tip-of-the-iceberg description of tools that you must see in pictures or in person to appreciate. I have used many of them since I was 10 without knowing their official names. I thought I would teach you their names before 25 years pass you by.

"If the only tool you have is a hammer, you tend to see every problem as a nail."
— *Abraham Maslow*

> *Use the right tool,*
> *Your papi*

 #117 THINGS I WISH I HAD TAUGHT MY SON… AND STILL CAN
The blinking cursor…

You have to write a paper for school and you sit down to get started. You figured you would get started when you sat down to write, but you haven't been thinking of your subject matter until now. And the cursor is just blinking… It's not helping.

Cursor is the Latin word for runner. Once you start running with it, the words come easy and you get into a flow. But right now, it's not running forward. It's running in place. It's like that lonely vacant motel sign that they often show in movies.

If you find yourself unable to get started don't just stare at the cursor. Try to go old school. Pull out a piece of paper or notebook and change your environment. I have a little 3 1/2 x 5 inch notebook that I always have with me.

If you need to go to the bathroom, do that now. If you're hungry, go eat. If you have to wash clothes, get on it. If there's a sunset outside, soak it in. Make sure you take your paper (or notebook) and something you can write with. Wait for the next wave.

I have no less than 15 full notebooks of what is called Mind Mapping. These look like spider drawings of random word and picture associations revolving around a subject or the subjects that revolve around that subject. I develop fun ideas, presentations, TV shows, business models, marketing campaigns, movies, songs and a whole bunch of other idea forms using this technique. I bought a book called *Mind Mapping* by Tony Buzon that provided me with a template. You can borrow it before you go back if you want to try this powerful form of ideation. As for the template, I've changed it to my taste. These spider charts are like branches connected to branches of ideas that pop into my head so that perhaps they will fit my project in some neat way. As opposed to drafting up an outline (which is linear), this Mind-Mapping approach is non-linear. I don't have to think of things in order.

By the time I sit down to write you every morning or night, I have already seen or felt or envisioned where this email will take me. Sometimes I have a general idea and I just go out into my mind's ocean with my writing surfboard and wait for the right wave to ride. I can't surf in the real world but I can certainly ride mind waves... Once I catch the right one, I can find myself inside a cool tube of thoughts. If I fall off, I just go back for another.

Finally, if you can't get started, just write a first sentence. Even if you hate it, you already got started and can go back to delete it. It's a not big deal. I have a whole mind landfill full of discarded first sentences. They were making my cursor trip.

> *Now get started,*
> *Your papi*

PS: I have found that when I really don't want to write because of laziness or fatigue...
      I end up doing a better job and having a more rewarding time.

 #118 THINGS I WISH I HAD TAUGHT MY SON... AND STILL CAN
The tools of the trade... Part 2.

Tongs, the first pliers, have been around since before the birth of Christ. Early metal workers used them in the process of smithing... To help them pull their metal item in and out of fire.

Hephaestus, the Greek god of fire, blacksmiths, craftsmen, artisans, sculptors, and metallurgy, is depicted in paintings with a pair of tongs…

Pliers are the handy tools I want to inform you about. I'm no expert in this department but I have used this tool(s) all my life. What are they for? For the times you have to grip something and your fingers just don't have the strength, pliers bring in the power. Their design converts the power of a hand's grip to a precision grip with concentrated power (the pliers that do this are called slip joint pliers). Slip joint pliers hold nuts (the metal kind) in place while you thread screws into them. They can twist or untwist wires. These pliers can also can assist you in bending or shaping a wire that is as thick as a clothes hanger or perhaps a bit thicker… And they have countless more uses.

There are specialized pliers that can help you complete an electrical work project (lineman's side-cutting pliers), reach hard-to-get-to places (needle-nose pliers which usually have a wire-cutting function too) and attaching things like RF cable terminals and Ethernet cable terminals to the end of cabling (crimping pliers). Cable and satellite installation guys use these crimping pliers when they wire a home.

Finally, I'll just mention a gotta-have plier called the locking plier which is often called a vice grip. This plier opens in adjustable sizes because it has a screw that you tighten or loosen to fit the project at hand. Once adjusted this plier clamps down like a pit bull and doesn't let go until you squeeze the release mechanism.

There are pictures of all these pliers at the following link. http://en.wikipedia.org/wiki/Pliers

When you are ready for a live demonstration of how these work in the real world, not the word world, let me know.

> *Now you can get a grip,*
> *Your papi*

 #119 THINGS I WISH I HAD TAUGHT MY SON… AND STILL CAN
Your life is like a jar…

There is an email that is circulating the world about how to set priorities. It is about rocks. Still, I imagine you probably haven't heard the insightful little story.

The story goes that a professor, in front of his class, pulls out a glass jar. He then fills the jar to the top with large rocks… Roughly baseball-sized rocks. The professor asks if it is full.

They all reply yes... It's full.

The professor then grabs pea-sized gravel and pours it in with the larger rocks. He shakes the glass jar until the gravel reaches under the big rocks and fills the container to the top. He then asks the class if the jar is now full.

"Yes," they say.

The professor then proceeds to add sand to the jar. It travels to the bottom slowly filling the jar, filling every available empty space.

"Now? Is it full?"

At this point, the students know that this is a trick question. Some say no... Some say yes.

The professor then pours water into the glass jar. It trickles down and slowly but surely, it fills the jar.

"What point am I trying to make?" the professor continues.

Somebody answers, "that no matter how busy we are, we can always fit more into our schedule?"

The professor says, "No! The lesson is PUT IN THE BIG ROCKS FIRST."

This little anecdote has morphed over the years. I don't know what meaning the original author intended this story to transfer. I can only offer what I think it means to me. I believe the story is about putting your most important priorities first... The big rocks. If you take care of the big rocks in your life, the gravel, sand and water will fit more easily. If you start with the smallest things, the big rocks (the big things you want in life) may not fit. In my life, my wife and family are my biggest rocks. For some people, their car or their career is their biggest rock. For me, I'm not sure if my past cars have been sand or water. Thank God because many of these material (gravel-like and sand-like) possessions are now either useless or worthless or both.

What will you fill your life jar with?

> *You rock!*
> *Your papi*

✉ #120 THINGS I WISH I HAD TAUGHT MY SON… AND STILL CAN
The way time spins…

I found this little story again today… It sounds like I wrote it to you back in the late 90s. I guess I was saving it for a later date. Perhaps you read it before. The email below says that I found and sent this little story on May 20th, 1998 to my parents, brothers and extended family (we were excited about the advent of email and were sending each other wonderful little memories back then). This is how the email read (with a few little interjections today from me):

Here is another story I can't remember writing. But it was here on my hard drive/computer. I guess it's better if I share it than let it gather digital dust.

THE MYSTERY OF TROMPOS

Titi was the best trompo spinner in the neighborhood. Loli, his brother, was the second best. They were the Guardian brothers. Together, they brought fear to us, the not-so-great trompo spinners.

(I'll interject here that trompos are wooden spinning tops that we customized with sharp nail points for combat. The object of the game of trompos (spinning top competition) that we played involved each of us trying to strike a blow to the top in the makeshift target area on the hard ground. We would forcefully throw our trompo (point down) at the target trompo on the ground and try to strike it (puncture it, break it). If on the thrust, the trompo was not stricken, then we had to pick up the spinning top before it lost its momentum and carefully tap the target trompo. Not doing this in time (before the top stopped spinning) resulted in your trompo now becoming the new target for the other strikers until somebody else missed.)

"Ya no juego! (I'm not playing anymore)"… Those were everybody's words when Titi and Loli Guardian would show up. Isacito ito would quit. Cüica would pull out. Jito and El Guero too… And they'd quit precisely when my trompo was in the bull-pin… While it was completely at the mercy of the Guardian brothers.

"Maybe I should cry and try to retrieve my hand-crafted double-headed, razor sharp pointed nail trompo decorated with Krylon, green and black paint," I told myself. "To hell with being called a crybaby. This is my pride and joy."

But I watched. I waited. Every single shot at my trompo felt like flesh being pulled from my bones. I cringed at near misses that would have parted my trompo in half had they struck with the punta.

I guess trompo contests were a kind of rite of passage in a small town in South Texas in the 70s. It taught you to take risks (That's a nice way to say gambling). It takes concentration, discipline, craftsmanship… Yeah sure! It helps if you have an older brother to design and customize your trompo and pull you out of tight spots. And it most certainly helps if you own a metal file to sharpen your point.

Playing trompos was like living out warrior fantasies. I can't decide what music soundtrack would fit a trompo competition… Maybe "Whip it" by Devo. I don't know. But I saw my green and black trompo a few days ago rolling around in my drawer. It was all dressed up for the final confrontation. It sorta looked like the Rambo of trompos. Fifteen years later, I'm not sure I can make it hum like I used to.

Can you spin a trompo (I guess I was writing to you)? Do you even know what it is? It is the Sega Mortal Kombat (Finish him!) of yesteryear. It is war. It was business. It was a form of gambling. It was the earliest stress I can remember. What happened to this art? Does anybody know why it just went away?

Did the Guardian brothers strike fear into everyone? Where are the Guardian brothers now?

I will tell you this… I saw my father "bailando a trompo" (spinning a top)… One of the many wonderful father and son experiences we had. He must have been more than 70 years old when he did this. I will never forget the momentary child in him… Coming out to play with me… (And I think you were there too).

I guess trompos were that powerful.

(End of trompo story)

What is the lesson for today? Save all your emails… They are your history. They are the modern day form of a diary. I have emails that date back to the early 90s, perhaps even before. Emails are only about two Kilobytes in size. There are 1,000 of those in one megabyte. And there are 1,000 megabytes in one gigabyte. In other words, they're small enough to store indefinitely for future reference. Nowadays, a four gigabyte jump drive can be bought for less than $20… A worthwhile price for protecting your history.

> *Maybe I'll try to find that trompo,*
> *Your papi*

TO THE THINGS I WISH I HAD TAUGHT MY SON...
AND STILL CAN READER

I began this journey not knowing that it would become a book(s)... It was just something to send to the email inbox of my son. Both of us are blessed that the blinking cursor on the screen kept moving forward and that important capsules of life poured out onto the screen. Somewhere in the process and at the suggestion of some readers, the book idea became an interesting next step to pursue. Because a thick book sometimes threatens readers (it used to threaten me), I decided to break these writings into three smaller books. Because this is an experiment, I wanted to keep costs low in case nobody actually bought the book.

If there is interest, there will be a second and third installment of these life lessons totaling 365 lessons to my son. If not... This will instantly become a collector's item.

I hope that you enjoyed this first book. I hope that you return to it to re-read some of the "things" that you found heart-warming, inspiring, helpful, etc.

Thank you from the bottom of the bottom of my heart.

> *To be continued...*
> *Jesús Ramírez*
> *jramirez@thestorytellingplace.com*

A FEW "THINGS" ABOUT ME...
TODAY...

In 2007 I began a new business venture preserving the life stories of senior citizens for their future generations. The company I started is called My Story. This project has finally gained traction and people are starting to consider the importance of leaving behind the gift of their story.

For more information, you can visit thestorytellingpalce.com. I am still creating brands, consulting on marketing projects, songwriting and pursuing Vuja Dé inventions (I release an iPhone app this month). A children's book about a prehistoric dragonfly is also swirling around in my head. As of the printing of this book (May 2010), my son is completing his second year in college.

My family loves me.

I thank God for life and for all my blessings.

www.ingramcontent.com/pod-product-compliance
Lightning Source LLC
Chambersburg PA
CBHW080422060326
40689CB00019B/4337